BRITAIN'S KINGS AND QUEENS

IN BITE-SIZED CHUNKS

Kevin Flude is the Creative Director of the Old Operating Theatre Museum in London and a lecturer at various universities. He has worked in the museum world for over thirty years, including the Museum of London and the Victoria and Albert Museum. He is also the Course Director for the Road Scholar programme in London, which provides study tours, lectures and walks on the history, archaeology and museums of the city.

BRITAIN'S KINGS AND QUEENS

IN BITE-SIZED CHUNKS

KEVIN FLUDE

Michael O'Mara Books Limited

First published under the title *Divorced, Beheaded, Died* in 2009
This edition first published in Great Britain in 2020 by
Michael O'Mara Books Limited
9 Lion Yard
Tremadoc Road
London SW4 7NQ

A CIP catalogue record for this book is available from the British Library.

Papers used by Michael O'Mara Books Limited are natural, recyclable
products made from wood grown in sustainable forests. The manufacturing
processes conform to the environmental regulations of the country of origin.

ISBN: 978-1-78929-234-3 in paperback print format
ISBN: 978-1-78929-277-0 in hardback print format

1 2 3 4 5 6 7 8 9 10

Designed and typeset by www.glensaville.com
Maps on pp.32 and 40 © Michael O'Mara Books Limited

Printed and bound by CPI Group (UK) Ltd, Croydon, CR0 4YY

www.mombooks.com

CONTENTS

To Connie and Hetty for making me proud.

Willie Willie Harry Stee
Harry Dick John Harry three;
One two three Neds, Richard two
Harrys four five six ... then who?
Edwards four five, Dick the bad,
Harrys (twain), Ned six (the lad);
Mary, Bessie, James you ken,
Then Charlie, Charlie, James again...
Will and Mary, Anna Gloria,
Georges four, Will four Victoria;
Edward seven next, and then
Came George the fifth in nineteen ten;
Ned the eighth soon abdicated
Then George six was coronated;
After which Elizabeth
And that's all folks until her death.

EDITORS' INTRODUCTION AND ACKNOWLEDGEMENTS

It is slightly unfashionable, these days, to be taught very much about the kings and queens of Britain. Those of us who have been educated the so-called 'modern' way have gone through our entire school career learning only a few disconnected facts about Henry VIII or Queen Victoria, with little idea of how they join up or why their stories are important. Those who experienced a more 'old-fashioned' education, by contrast, learned a great deal about the monarchy, much of it in the form of crushingly boring dates, facts and figures, and most of it promptly forgotten as soon as the exams were over.

There is a need, then, for this kind of book, one that places the monarchy firmly in its rightful place at the centre of British history yet delights in recounting the human stories of these remarkable men and women. For it is striking how often the personal influences the political in history – how the fate of the nation can hang on the whims and fancies of one person at the top. The most famous example is Henry VIII, who changed the entire country's official religion as a result of his determination to rid himself of his first wife. But in these pages you will find countless other examples, from King John's greed and lack of judgement, which led directly to the foundations of modern constitutional law, to Charles I's stubborn intransigence, which started a civil war. Although no historian worth his salt would claim that it is a monarch's personality alone that changes the course of history – no one, not even a king, exists in a vacuum – nonetheless it can play a hugely important role, as these stories show.

This book also offers the opportunity to place at centre stage the stories that are usually left in the margins, so there are sections on the important Welsh and Scottish monarchs, the legendary kings of ancient Britain, and the early British warlords, many of whose names are unfamiliar to us now but who between them mapped out the boundaries of what we now call Scotland, England and Wales. Through these stories we can see how the nation we know as 'Britain' came slowly – and often painfully – into being.

By deliberately keeping the entries in this book short and to the point, we hope to provide an accessible and entertaining overview of the sweep of British history that will perhaps renew a dormant interest in the subject amongst those readers who have not picked up a history book for a while, or ignite a spark for those who are hearing these stories for the first time. Either way, we hope you enjoy reading these 'bite-sized chunks' of history as much as we have enjoyed compiling them.

The editors would like to thank, first of all, Kevin Flude for his great breadth of knowledge as well as his eye for interesting detail. We would also like to thank Juliana Foster, Glen Saville, Judith Palmer, Ana Bjezancevic, Toby Buchan and Anna Marx for their important contributions in putting this book together, Connie Flude for additional royal research, and Thomas Edlin for his invaluable fact-checking and historical input. Needless to say, any remaining errors are our own.

LEGENDARY KINGS OF BRITAIN

ॐ

B ritain does not pay much attention to its mythological origins or legendary kings. The main source of our knowledge is the writings of Geoffrey of Monmouth, in particular his *History of the Kings of Britain*, which first appeared around AD 1136. Monmouth loved a good story more than he cared for historical accuracy, and as a consequence reputable English historians tend to dismiss the stories and pass them over to their literary colleagues. But these are our foundation myths and should be treasured, just as we treasure stories of Romulus and Remus, and Odysseus and Achilles.

BRUTUS
Reigned *c.* 1160–1137 BC

Brutus, according to legend, was the first king of Britain and gave his name to the island (Brutus was his Latinized name; contemporaries would have known him as Brut or Brit). He was a Trojan descended from Aeneas, who survived the sack of Troy and whose descendant Romulus founded Rome.

Brutus led a group of Trojans to Britain where they wiped out the native inhabitants, a race of giants. The last giant standing was Gogmagog, who met his end in a wrestling match with the warrior Corineus, one of Brutus's companions. Corineus went on to be the first Duke of Cornwall, while Brutus set up his capital, Troia Nova (New Troy), on the banks of the Thames, which later became the site of London. It was here that Brutus is said to have been buried twenty-three years after arriving in Britain.

BLADUD
Reigned *c.* 937–917 BC

A couple of hundred years later, the heir to the throne, Prince Bladud, contracted leprosy and was banished from the royal court. Earning a living as a humble pig herd on the banks of the River

Avon, he noticed that his pigs were cured of their skin complaints after rolling around in the mud near some hot springs. Bladud followed suit and was cured of his leprosy. He was welcomed back to court, and in time became king. He founded Bath near the site of his miraculous cure and became a renowned necromancer, experimenting with elemental forces. Determined to conquer the air, he made himself a pair of wings and soared over New Troy (now called Trinovantum) but lost control and crashed down on to the Temple of Apollo and was killed.

LEIR
Reigned *c.* 917–857 BC

Bladud's son, King Leir, made famous by Shakespeare's dramatized version of his life, ruled for sixty years. In his old age, Leir wanted to divide his kingdom among his three daughters, but decided to test their love. Regan and Goneril flattered the old King and received a share of the kingdom, but his favourite and youngest daughter, Cordelia, would only say that she loved him as a daughter ought to love her father. Furious, Leir forced her into exile. However, he was gradually stripped of his power by Regan and Goneril, and finally he fled to France, where his youngest daughter was now married to the King of the Franks. Cordelia treated him with respect and his honour was restored. Together they won back the kingdom, and Leir regained the throne for the last three years of his life. After his death, Cordelia ruled Britain for five years before being imprisoned by the sons of her sisters. She could not bear the loss of her kingdom and committed suicide in prison.

LUD
Reigned *c.* 73–58 BC

King Lud is said to have been the brother of Cassivellaunus, who led the defence against Julius Caesar's second attempt to invade Britain in 54 BC. Lud rebuilt the city of Trinovantum with magnificent new walls, huge towers and splendid palaces. The city was renamed Caer Lud or Lud Dun (Lud's Fort) and later became London. It is said the King was buried at Ludgate.

THE WARRIOR KINGS AND QUEENS OF BRITAIN

❧

When the Romans arrived in the first century BC, Britain was inhabited by people who spoke a dialect of the Celtic language and who claimed to be indigenous. The country was divided into various territories, each ruled by a king or queen. Apart from legends, we know little about these early rulers, but when Julius Caesar first attempted to invade Britain in 55 BC, events began to be reported in written accounts for a Roman audience and a clearer picture begins to emerge of the warrior kings and queens of Britain.

CASSIVELLAUNUS
Reigned *c.* 54 BC

Cassivellaunus was a king of the Catuvellauni tribe, whose kingdom centred on what is now Hertfordshire. Although the exact dates of his reign are not known, Cassivellaunus is first mentioned as the leader of the combined British defence forces against Julius Caesar's second invasion of Britain in 54 BC. Although he failed to defeat Caesar in open battle, his use of guerrilla tactics led to Caesar abandoning his conquest after a face-saving battle, and the Roman legions did not return to Britain for another nine decades. He appears as a heroic, almost godlike figure, Caswallon, in the medieval Welsh stories, the *Mabinogion*.

CUNOBELINUS
Reigned *c.* AD 10–41

By Cunobelinus's time, the territory of the Catuvellauni had been combined with that of their neighbouring tribe, the Trinovantes (Essex), and their capital had moved to what is now Colchester. Cunobelinus was a master of diplomacy, and he kept Rome on his side despite extending his power over most of south-eastern Britain. The Roman historian Tacitus gave him the title of *Britannorum Rex* and his coins have been discovered across England and Wales, so he can therefore claim to be the first recognized king of Britain. Because of these good relations with Rome, his reign saw a substantial increase in trade with the continent, with many luxury goods such as wine and olive oil being imported. Shakespeare based his play *Cymbeline* on Cunobelinus, although there are not many similarities between fact and fiction.

CARATACUS
Reigned *c.* AD 41–51

On the death of Cunobelinus, two of his sons, Caratacus and Togodumnus, took over his territory. Their aggressive attacks on the neighbouring kingdom of the Atrebates (Hampshire) led their king, Verica, to seek Roman protection, giving Emperor Claudius an excuse to invade in AD 43. Within a short while, Togodumnus was killed and Caratacus had lost his kingdom. But he did not give up, and led a staunch and bloody campaign against the Romans for several years. Finally, the Romans forced a pitched battle in Wales in AD 51 and Caratacus was defeated, although he managed to escape. He attempted to persuade the large northern tribe of the Brigantes to join the anti-Roman resistance, but was betrayed by their queen, Cartimandua, and handed over to the Romans. He was due to be executed, but his bravery and bearing led to a pardon and the freedom to live out the rest of his life in Rome. Welsh legend remembers him as Caradog.

BOUDICCA
Reigned *c.* AD 60

The wealthy King Prasutagus of the Iceni (based in East Anglia) had a policy of peace with the Romans. He died in around AD 60, whereupon the Romans revoked Icenian independence, seized Iceni territory and recalled their loans. Prasutagus's widow, Boudicca (or Boadicea as she is sometimes known), was flogged and their two daughters were raped.

In revenge, Boudicca led the attack against the Romans with extraordinary brutality. She initially met with outstanding success, destroying the Ninth Legion and burning down the three leading Roman towns – Camulodunum (Colchester), Londinium and Verulamium (St Albans) – killing an estimated 80,000 people. But perhaps she became over-confident. The Roman governor, Gaius Suetonius Paullinus, and his two legions returned from attacking the druids in Anglesey and destroyed Boudicca's army, despite being vastly outnumbered. Boudicca is said to have committed suicide, and according to popular legend she is buried under Platform 9 of Kings Cross Station. The Romans gradually regained the initiative and Roman rule continued for over 300 years.

COGIDUBNUS
Died *c.* AD 80

In Chichester there is a Roman inscription dedicated to the 'Great King of Britain', Tiberius Claudius Cogidubnus. His Roman names are the names of Emperor Claudius, suggesting that he, or perhaps his father, helped the Romans during the invasion, possibly assisting the future Emperor Vespasian to reduce British resistance in the west. Roman historian Tacitus records that after the Roman conquest Cogidubnus was given control of several territories and remained loyal to the Romans until his death. At Fishbourne, outside Chichester, there is a fabulous Roman palace that might have been his.

LUCIUS
Reigned *c.* AD 124–201

Although King Lucius's name is recorded by the Venerable Bede, one of the most reliable early historians, there has been great reluctance to accord Lucius historical status. Vatican records reported that Pope Eleutherius received a letter from Lucius requesting to be made a Christian. It is therefore possible that he was Britain's first Christian king, although some have suggested that the papal record contains a typographical error and actually referenced a king of Edessa. Lucius is said to have reigned for over seventy years, and to have founded St Peter Upon Cornhill in the City of London in AD 179, though both seem unlikely to archaeologists.

EMPERORS WHO RULED FROM BRITAIN

෪

Roman rule in Britain was established by Emperor Claudius's successful invasion in AD 43. On arrival, they met with fierce resistance from some of Britain's Celtic tribal leaders, especially in the west, but others allied themselves with their Roman conquerors and became client-kings, leading to dynasties of Romano-British rulers. By the end of the first century, most of the resistance had died down, and Roman control continued until the early fifth century. A handful of the Roman leaders were created Emperor while in Britain, and have a special relationship with Britain that, in one way or another, means Britain can stake a claim to them.

ALBINUS
Reigned *c.* AD 193–197

Decimus Clodius Septimius Albinus was governor of Britain in AD 193 when Emperor Pertinax was murdered. There were three claimants to the throne: Albinus, Septimius Severus and Niger. All three men had control of various legions that were scattered around the empire, which led to all three being declared emperor. Severus initially allied himself with Albinus and turned his attention towards Niger, whom he defeated in AD 194. He then betrayed his ally and Albinus was defeated and executed in AD 197.

CARAUSIUS
Reigned *c.* AD 286–293

Marcus Aurelius Mausaeus Carausius gained success as a general in northern France, and was given the task of eliminating Saxon pirates from Roman waters. He was accused of keeping the pirates' booty for himself, however, and was condemned to death. Refusing to accept his sentence, he gathered together an army and declared himself emperor of Britain and northern France. His military and diplomatic skills were so great that his rule was largely uncontested by Rome. But in AD 293 he was murdered by his financial officer, Allectus, who took over as emperor. This spin-off empire lasted another three years, until Allectus was killed by troops of Constantius Chlorus, father of Constantine the Great, and Britain was reunited with the Roman Empire.

CONSTANTINE THE GREAT
Reigned AD 306–337

Flavius Valerius Aurelius Constantinus was proclaimed emperor in York on the death of his father, Constantius Chlorus, in AD 306. The appointment was hotly disputed and it was not until AD 324 that he defeated the last of his rivals and his position was finally secured. He was the first Christian Roman emperor and his policy of religious tolerance led to the AD 313 Edict of Milan, which forbade persecution on the grounds of religion. He built a magnificent city on the site of the ancient city of Byzantium, named it Constantinople and declared it the new capital of the Roman Empire. Although he did not spend much time in Britain, he is linked to the country by the legend that his mother, Helen, was the daughter of the mythical Old King Cole. Whatever the truth of this, he is undoubtedly an important figure in the history of Britain because he was responsible for paving the way to Christianity's widespread acceptance in the country.

MAGNUS MAXIMUS
Reigned *c*. AD 383–388

Magnus Maximus was an experienced soldier from Spain who was appointed a count of Britain. In AD 383 he was proclaimed emperor by his troops and took legions out of Britain to consolidate his control of the western empire, thus weakening Britain's defences. There is some evidence that he recruited barbarian tribes to defend the western coastline of Britain, as several Welsh dynasties (Powys, Gwent, Dyfed) begin their family tree with Macsen Wledig, thought to be the local name for Magnus. He is also thought to have begun the settlement of British people in Brittany. Despite a solid reputation as emperor, Magnus soon lost power and was executed.

THE END OF ROMAN BRITAIN
AD 407–411

In AD 406–7 the Roman Empire was assailed by a series of barbarian invasions and Roman troops were withdrawn from Britain to protect the empire's heartland. In AD 407 local British troops seized their opportunity to rebel and declared a soldier, Marcus, emperor. He did not live up to expectations, however, and he was killed later that same year. Power then passed to a local British aristocrat, Gratian. His too was a short-lived reign and he was murdered after only four months, when he refused the army permission to attack the barbarians in Gaul.

Flavius Claudius Constantinus, a talented soldier, was then proclaimed Emperor Constantine III, or Constantine II of Britain. Constantine immediately went on the offensive and took all available troops to the continent to wrestle for control of the empire. Despite some considerable initial success, Constantine and his troops were eventually overwhelmed and he surrendered and was beheaded in AD 411. But Rome was greatly weakened by the events of the past few years, and Roman rule ended after Constantine's death.

DARK-AGE
WARLORD KINGS

☙

When the Romans left Britain in 410, Britain was vulnerable to attack from Ireland, Scotland and Germany. The most serious threat came from the Germanic races of the Angles, Saxons, Jutes and Frisians, who invaded and initially settled in areas around the east coast, but then began to push northwards and westwards, driving the Celts into Cornwall, Wales and parts of the north. They were fiercely resisted, and the Battle of Mount Badon in the early 500s stopped the Germanic invasions for a generation or two.

VORTIGERN
Reigned *c.* **425–460s**

There are few certain sources of information concerning Vortigern, but it seems that he came to power during a time when Britain was under threat from the Picts and Caledonians in the north, the Gaelic Scotti tribe in Ireland, and the Germanic tribes in the east, filling the power vacuum left by the Romans' departure. It is said that Vortigern made the decision to invite the Saxons to come over as mercenaries and settle in certain parts of Britain, asking in return that they help to defeat the other raiders. This policy was initially successful, but eventually the Saxon newcomers, led by legendary leaders Hengist and Horsa, rebelled and took over more territory, with Hengist declaring himself King of Kent. It was thus that Britain's first Anglo-Saxon kingdom was established, and Vortigern came to be remembered as the architect of Britain's betrayal.

AMBROSIUS AURELIANUS
Reigned *c.* **460s**

Little is known about Ambrosius Aurelianus, though some have speculated that he was in fact the legendary King Arthur. Aurelianus has also been called 'the last of the Romans' due to his Roman ancestry, and was possibly even a descendant of one of the emperors. He is said to have been a sworn enemy of Vortigern, the leader who invited the dreaded Saxons into Britain, as his parents were killed by the Saxon marauders. He later rallied British forces against the Anglo-Saxon advance and met with some success.

RIOTHAMUS
Reigned *c*. 470

A sixth-century writer refers to one Riothamus as 'King of the Britons' when describing a battle against the Goths in France. Very little else is known about Riothamus, and it has been suggested that the name is a Latinization of an old British word meaning 'supreme king'. This in turn has led to speculation that Riothamus may not have existed and might simply be another name for Vortigern, Ambrosius Aurelianus or even the elusive King Arthur.

ARTHUR
Reigned *c*. late fifth century–early sixth century

The trouble with King Arthur is that there is no contemporary, or even near contemporary, evidence that he ever really existed. The story of a British king or warlord who led the Christian Britons against the pagan Saxons fits with what we know of events in the fifth and sixth centuries; the story of Arthur leading an expedition to France and taking on the Romans fits the story of Constantine the Great, Magnus Maximus, Constantine III and Riothamus. So we don't really know whether Arthur is a mythological composite hero or a real person. His association with legends in Brittany,

Cornwall, Somerset, Wales and Scotland is either evidence that he is mythic or that he fought the Saxons wherever they showed their heads.

If he did exist, he was probably a general who controlled a highly trained cavalry force. He is said to have fought twelve great victorious battles leading up to the great battle at Mount Badon in around 518, which saw the Saxons so comprehensively defeated that peace broke out for a generation or more. Although the Battle of Mount Badon undoubtedly took place, Arthur's name is not mentioned in the earliest sources.

According to legend, the Arthurian golden age continued until the treachery of his nephew, Modred, led to a terrible battle at Camlann at which Arthur was mortally wounded and taken off to the magical island of Avalon, never to be heard of alive again. Whatever the truth, a generation or so after the Battle of Mount Badon, the Saxons continued their advance, securing the Anglo-Saxon domination of England which has lasted to the present day.

BRETWALDAS – RULERS OF ANGLO-SAXON BRITAIN

꩜

As the Angles, Saxons, Jutes and Frisians (collectively known as the English or Anglo-Saxons) increasingly made inroads on the old Roman province of Britain, Roman civilization was destroyed and a new language and ethnic identity were forged. The English formed themselves into eight kingdoms. The Saxons claimed Essex, Wessex and Sussex; the Angles formed East Anglia, Mercia, and Bernicia and Deira (together known as Northumbria); and the Jutes claimed Kent. Some of the rulers of these new kingdoms became so powerful that their authority extended beyond their own lands and they were known as Bretwaldas (overkings).

AELLE OF SUSSEX
Reigned *c.* 477–514

The first Saxon leaders to set up kingdoms in England were Aelle (Sussex), Hengist and Horsa (Kent), and Cerdic and Cynric (West Saxon or Wessex). According to the historian Bede, Aelle was the first to gain Bretwalda or overking status, although it is difficult to see how this can be, given the weak toehold the Saxons had in Britain at the time and the small size of his kingdom.

Map showing Anglo-Saxon kingdoms c. 600 AD

CEAWLIN OF WESSEX
Reigned *c*. 560–591

Ceawlin was the grandson of Cerdic, the legendary founder of the West Saxon (Wessex) kingdom, and he became its third king. Few details are known of his life, but he seems to have taken advantage of the end of the peace established by the Battle of Mount Badon, when the invading Saxons were temporarily routed. His armies defeated three British kings – Coinmail, Condidan and Farinmail – at the pivotal Battle of Dyrham, taking Gloucester, Cirencester and Bath. This divided the Britons of Devon and Cornwall from the Britons of Wales and the north, and probably marked the end of any realistic British hope of getting rid of the English once and for all. Ceawlin's name, and that of his grandfather Cerdic, seem to be Celtic in origin, suggesting the tantalizing possibility that Wessex was originally an alliance between the English and Britons.

AETHELBERHT OF KENT
Reigned *c*. 591–616

Aethelberht claimed descent from Hengist and Horsa, who had seized Kent from the Britons, and became the third Bretwalda. The Kentish kingdom had close ties to France and Aethelberht married the Christian daughter of the King of France, Bertha, whose marriage settlement allowed her freedom of worship. Pope Gregory sent a very reluctant Augustine to Britain to begin the conversion of the English to Christianity, and within a short time of Augustine's arrival in Kent Aethelberht had been converted, thus becoming the first of the Anglo-Saxon Christian kings. In around

602, he composed a code of laws, possibly the first document written in Anglo-Saxon.

RAEDWALD OF EAST ANGLIA
Reigned *c.* 600–624

King Raedwald of East Anglia was baptized as a Christian during a visit to King Aethelberht in Kent. But his attitude to the new religion was ambivalent at best, and on his return to East Anglia he quickly slipped back into his pagan ways. He did set up a Christian altar, but in a temple where sacrifices to pagan gods continued. Raedwald defeated the Northumbrians at the Battle of the River Idle in Nottinghamshire in 616, thus becoming the first Bretwalda to hold sway north of the Humber.

In 1939, at Sutton Hoo, a seventh-century ship burial containing a host of treasures was excavated. Magnificent weapons and armour, fabulous feasting equipment and other royal paraphernalia were uncovered. The mix of pagan and Christian artifacts found at Sutton Hoo suggests that this great treasure belonged to Raedwald, and that even in death he continued to hedge his bets.

EDWIN
Reigned *c.* 616–633

In the north, Edwin of Deira was exiled by King Aethelfrith of Bernicia, who united the two kingdoms as Northumbria. Aethelfrith was a pagan who slaughtered his British Christian enemies with abandon. At the Battle of Chester in 614 he is said to have slaughtered 1,200 British monks, arguing that they were combatants as they supported their army with prayer. In 616 he was defeated by King Raedwald of East Anglia, who gave Northumbria to Edwin.

King Edwin completed the conquest of the local British kingdoms, securing Northumbria's domination of the north. In 625 he married Aethelburga, sister of the Christian King of Kent, and converted to Christianity, and by 627 he was the most powerful of the Anglo-Saxon kings.

In 633 Edwin was killed by the combined armies of Penda, the pagan Anglo-Saxon King of Mercia, and the British King Cadwallon of Gwynedd at the Battle of Hatfield Chase.

OSWALD
Reigned *c.* 634–642

Oswald was the son of Aethelfrith, who united two kingdoms as Northumbria. When his father was killed, Oswald was exiled to Ireland, where he converted to Christianity. When the new King of Northumbria, Edwin, was defeated by the British King Cadwallon, Northumbria was again split into two. Oswald returned from exile with an army, defeated Cadwallon, reunited Northumbria, and spread Christianity throughout the land. Oswald was killed in 642 by the pagan King Penda of Mercia at the Battle of Maserfield, where his body was dismembered and hung on a tree. He is now venerated as a Christian saint.

OSWY
Reigned *c.* 642–670

When his brother Oswald was defeated and killed by the pagan King Penda of Mercia, Oswy became King of Bernicia. He married his daughter to the son of Penda, who became a Christian, and also persuaded the King of Essex to convert. Despite these diplomatic efforts, in 655 Penda invaded with a massive army, but Oswy unexpectedly defeated and killed him at the Battle of Winwaed (near Leeds), a victory which secured his status as a Bretwalda.

Concerned by the differences in religious practices between the Christian Celtic Church and the Roman Church, Oswy called the famous Synod at Whitby in 664 to decide the issue. It was agreed that the Roman traditions should be followed, thus confirming England's status as a Roman Catholic country, which was to remain unchanged for the next 700 years.

AETHELBALD
Reigned *c.* 716–757

Although Aethelbald of Mercia was not named as 'Bretwalda' this is probably because of prejudice on the part of the Saxon sources. Mercia (in the Midlands) developed from a series of small groupings of peoples including the Middle Angles and British tribes such as the Hwicce of Tewkesbury. King Penda (d. 655) put Mercia on the map until his aggression was ended by the Northumbrians. His son, Peada (d. 656), introduced Christianity, while Aethelbald was the first Mercian king to control all of England except Northumbria, and was therefore called Rex Britanniae ('King of Britain' in Latin). The Church accused him of being a lecher and adulterer, violating even nuns. He was murdered by his bodyguard.

OFFA
Reigned *c.* 757–796

Offa was King of Mercia, by far the most important kingdom in the eighth century. He took advantage of instability in various other kingdoms, and took control of Kent, Sussex and East Anglia, thereby subjecting most of Britain to his rule by the 780s. He corresponded with Emperor Charlemagne of France as an equal, and re-introduced coinage to Britain in order to trade with the Frankish empire. His power and influence were so great that he even managed to force the Church to create a new Mercian archdiocese in Lichfield. One of his greatest achievements was to build a huge dyke along the border with Wales as a defence against the Welsh tribes. After Offa's reign, the kings of Mercia continued to be the leading monarchs in Britain until the time of King Egbert of Wessex, at which point Wessex came to dominate.

EGBERT
Reigned 802–839

King Egbert was descended from Cerdic, the founder of the Wessex dynasty, and is claimed as the eighth Bretwalda. He undertook a savage attack on the Cornish and then he defeated the Mercians at the Battle of Ellendun near Swindon, and took control of Sussex, Surrey, Essex and Kent. Soon, Northumbria also submitted to his overlordship. However, his control of Britain was challenged by the coming of the Vikings – a group of fierce seafaring Norsemen from Scandinavia who began raiding Britain from 787 onwards.

ALFRED
Reigned 871–899

Alfred must have had little hope of becoming King of Wessex as he had three older brothers, though they each in turn died shortly after taking the throne. The crown passed to Alfred as his brother Aethelred I's children were too young to take power at such a dangerous time: by 871 Alfred's kingdom was the only one that had not fallen to the Vikings and it was in an extremely precarious position. In January 878 Wessex was attacked and Alfred was forced to flee in disguise to the Somerset marshes. It was here that, according to legend, he stayed with a peasant woman who asked him to mind the cakes she was cooking. Alfred, wrapped up in his plans to save England, let the cakes burn. He received his scolding most humbly – before revealing his true identity.

Alfred used his time in the marshes well, observing the tactics of the Vikings and gathering his forces. In May 878 he defeated the Danes at the Battle of Ethandune (or Edington), one of the most important battles ever held on British soil. One of Alfred's masterstrokes was to marry his daughter Aethelfleda to Aethelred, the heir to the throne of Mercia, which enabled the two territories to fight a united war against the Danes. With this force, Alfred was able to impose a peace treaty on the Danes that saw England divided in two: the English south and west, and the Viking north and east (known as 'Danelaw'). The leader of the Danes, Guthrum, agreed to convert to Christianity and took the name Aethelstan on baptism.

To consolidate his kingdom, Alfred established the navy, reorganized the army and set in motion a programme of building fortified settlements, known as *burhs* (boroughs). He rebuilt Winchester, which became the capital of Wessex and later England. He encouraged the arts and education by importing scholars, and developed the English language by translating parts of the Bible into English. He liberated kingdoms conquered by the Danes and kept them for himself, thus earning the title 'King of the English'. His extraordinary achievements are the reason why he remains the only English king to be given the sobriquet 'the Great'.

EDWARD THE ELDER
Reigned 899–924

Alfred's son had a disputed succession, as his cousin Aethelwold also claimed the throne. Edward defeated Aethelwold, who fled but returned with a Danish army. Aethelwold and Eohric, King of the East Anglian Danes, were among the notables slaughtered by Edward's army at a bloody battle in Cambridgeshire in 901. Edward followed this up by defeating the Northumbrian Vikings.

Edward's sister Aethelfleda and her husband, Aethelred, controlled Mercia and the west, while Edward extended his kingdom to the east and the north. After the death of her husband, Aethelfleda, a great warrior queen, took over as 'Lady of the Mercians'. Together she and Edward continued Alfred's policy of building fortified settlements, which proved very effective against the Danes. Aethelfleda won the boroughs of Derby and Leicester and defeated the Welsh, and Edward reconquered East Anglia and the east Midlands.

When Aethelfleda died, Edward took over direct control of Mercia, and by 922 most of Britain was under the control of one ruler for the first time since the end of the Roman occupation.

SAXON KINGS OF ENGLAND

ॐ

Although Alfred and his son Edward, Saxon Kings of Wessex, controlled a large part of the old Roman province of Britain, it was Alfred's grandson Aethelstan who was the first king to control all of England. The name England derived from the Angles, the Germanic people who had settled in the north and the Midlands in the fifth century. The great historian the Venerable Bede, writing in the eighth century, used it for his *Ecclesiastical History of the English People*. The names 'England' and 'the English' became unifying terms, so that when the kings of Wessex conquered the old kingdoms of Mercia and Northumbria, the new name became useful as it made them seem to be liberators rather than conquerors.

AETHELSTAN
Reigned 924–939

Aethelstan extended English control to the Viking kingdom of York, conquered Cornwall, and received homage from the kings of Wales and Scotland. He achieved his pre-eminence at the Battle of Brunanburh in 937, where he defeated a confederacy of the Scottish, Welsh, Norse and Irish and secured the title 'King of all Britain'. It is often claimed that it was not until Aethelstan's reign that an English monarchy was finally established. Aethelstan never married, but he arranged splendid marriages for his many sisters and half-sisters, so that he was connected with the courts of France, Burgundy, Aquitaine and Germany.

EDMUND I
Reigned 939–946

Edmund was Aethelstan's half-brother. He had to fight to retain his crown. Early in his reign, the Vikings recaptured York, but he was later able to bring it back under Saxon control. He extended his power by conquering Strathclyde and signing a treaty with King Malcolm I of Scotland, and he also received the submission of the Prince of Gwynedd. He was murdered, at the age of just twenty-four, by an outlaw named Liofa, while he was at a feast. As his children were still very young, he was succeeded by his brother Eadred.

EADRED
Reigned 946–955

Eadred had to struggle to subdue the Vikings in York. Although York was supposedly under Saxon control, they appointed the formidable Viking Eric Bloodaxe as their ruler, and Eadred was forced to take action. Eric was defeated in 954, and Eadred expelled the Danes from England and was designated 'King of the Anglo-Saxons, Northumbrians, Pagans and Britons'.

EADWIG
Reigned 955–959

Eadwig (or Edwy) was the eldest son of King Edmund and succeeded his uncle Eadred to the throne when he was just fifteen years old. He was nicknamed 'the Fair' due to his good looks, but his reign began with scandal when he was accused of a threesome with his eventual wife, Elgiva, and her mother, Ethelgiva. It is said that St Dunstan, the Abbot of Glastonbury, had to drag him back from their bed to his coronation celebration. Dunstan was exiled and the King married Elgiva, but the Church later forced an annulment on the grounds that they were close cousins and Elgiva was banished. Eadwig lost Mercia and Northumbria to his brother Edgar in a revolt, and his premature death in 959 averted a civil war.

EDGAR
Reigned 959–975

L ike his brother Eadwig, Edgar had his own idea of royal behaviour. He had relationships with several women and there were disputes as to which were wives and which merely concubines. It is said that he abducted a nun, St Wulfrida, the Abbess of Wilton, with whom he had an illegitimate child.

Despite this behaviour, Edgar's reign was remarkably peaceful, thus earning him the sobriquet 'the Peaceable'. Among his achievements are the development of the local government system of shires, which lasted until the late twentieth century, and the rebuilding of the monastic system, achieved with the help of his chief advisor, St Dunstan, now Archbishop of Canterbury, who had refused to crown him until he improved his conduct. He was only officially crowned fourteen years after coming to the throne, in a ceremony designed by Dunstan, the basic structure of which providing the model used ever since.

EDWARD
Reigned 975–978

B ecause of King Edgar's confused love life, the succession to the throne was not clear, but his son Edward, born in 962, was successful in staking his claim. His reign was short-lived, and he was murdered in Corfe Castle, possibly at the hands of his step-mother, Elfrida, his half-brother Aethelred's mother. After his death, Edward was declared a martyr and a saint.

AETHELRED II
Reigned 978–1016

Aethelred succeeded his half-brother to the throne while still a young boy. He was a warrior king who spent most of his life desperately trying to keep his English kingdom together in the face of renewed Viking attacks. One disastrous tactic he used was to buy off the Danish raiders using a tax called the Danegeld. This set up a sorry sequence: defeat in battle, payments to the victorious raiders and a few months of uneasy peace followed by the raiders seeking further and larger payments. Under this threat, the glue that held England together threatened to loosen. Earls of the old kingdoms saw the opportunity for independence, and treason posed as great a danger as the raiders.

In 1002 an increasingly desperate Aethelred ordered the slaughter of all Danes in his kingdom. One of the victims was the sister of King Swein of Denmark. This was one factor that led Swein to take a personal interest in the conquest of England, and by the end of 1013 Aethelred was in exile and Swein was on the throne. On Swein's death a few months later, Aethelred was briefly restored to the throne until his death in 1016, when he was succeeded by his son Edmund. His unfortunate reign led to the nickname 'the Ill-advised', sometimes translated as 'the Unready'.

EDMUND II
Reigned 1016

Edmund Ironside, as he was nicknamed, was born in around 988. He was crowned in 1016, on the death of his father, Aethelred the Unready. He was a formidable warrior and although he was defeated in battle by King Cnut, the son of King Swein of Denmark, his military prowess won him a peace treaty in which England was divided between the two kings. Unfortunately, Edmund died unexpectedly a few weeks later, his two children, Edward 'the Atheling' and Edmund, were exiled to Hungary. Cnut therefore claimed the whole of England by right of conquest.

THE VIKING KINGS OF ENGLAND

❧

The Vikings of Scandinavia had been raiding Britain since the 780s, sacking the famous monastery at Lindisfarne in 793. The Vikings soon began to settle, and progressively defeated the English kingdoms. The Danish leader Guthrum made a famous peace treaty with Alfred that set him up as ruler of eastern England, or 'Danelaw' as it became known. He ended up effectively as King of East Anglia. In the north the Vikings established the Kingdom of Jorvic (or York) that ruled Northumbria. Its last king was the murderous Eric Bloodaxe, who was ousted by King Eadred after murdering several half-brothers in a colourful career. There was a lull in attacks in the tenth century but in the early eleventh century the Vikings came back in force. King Aethelred and King Edmund desperately fought to maintain England's independence but England fell under the control of King Swein ('Forkbeard') of Denmark, whose son Cnut became the first Viking King of all England.

CNUT
Reigned 1016–1035

Cnut, or Canute, was born in around 995 and was the son of King Swein of Denmark. When Edmund II died in 1016, he became uncontested King of England by right of conquest and went on to become King of Denmark in 1018 and King of Norway in 1028. He consolidated his claim to England by killing or banishing his Saxon rivals and marrying Emma of Normandy, the widow of Aethelred II, with whom he had three children. He also had two illegitimate children by his first 'handfast' wife, Elgiva.

Although he was undoubtedly ruthless, he was a strong ruler. He deposed many of the aristocrats who governed England, but he was relatively open-handed in replacing them, so he had devoted English followers. He also allowed English laws to continue and sought good relationships with the Church.

The famous tale of Cnut setting up his throne on the seashore and commanding the tide to turn, to no avail, was an attempt to demonstrate to sycophantic courtiers the limits of his power, and may have taken place in London, on the banks of the tidal Thames.

HAROLD I
Reigned 1037–1040

Harold was the illegitimate son of King Cnut by his concubine, Elgiva. He was nicknamed 'Harold Harefoot' because he was fleet of foot and loved hunting. On his father's death in 1035, Harold was appointed regent, as his half-brother Harthacnut, the recognized heir to Cnut's throne, was busy in Denmark. Unhappy with his regent status, Harold usurped the throne in 1037, but died in 1040, just as Harthacnut was preparing an invasion to reclaim his throne.

HARTHACNUT
Reigned 1040–1042

Harthacnut was the son of King Cnut and his second wife, Emma of Normandy. He succeeded as King of England and Denmark on his father's death in 1035, but the English throne was usurped by his half-brother Harold. Harold died in 1040, and Harthacnut was crowned at Canterbury Cathedral. He was a deeply unpopular king who raised taxes to such an extent that Lady Godiva felt it necessary to ride naked through Coventry to protest against the taxation of the townspeople. Harthacnut was unmarried and so invited his half-brother, Edward the Confessor, son of Emma and her first husband Aethelred the Unready, to return from exile and become heir to the throne. He died very suddenly from a seizure after a drinking session.

THE LAST KINGS OF ANGLO-SAXON ENGLAND

❧

The deaths of the dreadful Viking sons of Cnut allowed the return of the royal English bloodline in the form of King Edward the Confessor, after he had waited twenty years in exile in Normandy. England was at this time almost a confederation of regions with different ethnic backgrounds: the Vikings were represented strongly in the east and the north, the Britons in the west and the English in-between. The aristocracy was referred to as 'Anglo-Danish' as the English and the Danish Vikings intermarried. Typical was Earl Godwin, an English aristocrat who made two advantageous marriages to Danes, firstly to King Cnut's sister and then to a granddaughter of another King of Denmark. Their son Harold became the last English King.

EDWARD THE CONFESSOR
Reigned 1042–1066

Edward was the son of Aethelred II and Emma of Normandy, and was born in around 1003. He was exiled to Normandy during the reign of the Viking kings, but was recalled by his half-brother King Harthacnut and became heir to the throne.

On Harthacnut's death, Edward faced many difficulties in restoring the English monarchy, the most dangerous being the number of contenders for the English throne. Edward did not help matters in this respect, as there is evidence that he offered the succession to the Kings of Denmark and Norway, and his cousin William of Normandy also claimed that he had been made heir. Furthermore, Edward's marriage in 1045 to Edith, the daughter of Earl Godwin of Wessex, boosted the already enormously powerful Godwin clan's aspirations to the throne. Edward could have resolved all this by producing an heir, but he and Edith had no children. Indeed, there were rumours that the marriage was never consummated.

Edward's reign was made difficult by the powerful position of the Godwin family, which threatened civil war. Earl Godwin was implicated in the blinding and murder of Edward's brother, Alfred, and was involved in several armed conflicts with the King. But by the end of his reign, Edward seems to have reconciled with the clan as Godwin's son, Harold, was declared heir to the throne.

Edward's reign was relatively peaceful and he oversaw some successes against the Welsh and the Scots, with his nominee Malcolm, for example, achieving the overthrow of Macbeth with English support.

A deeply pious man, Edward built the magnificent Westminster Abbey (though none of his building remains), where he was buried on his death in 1066. He was made a saint in 1161.

HAROLD II
Reigned 1066

Harold Godwinson was King Edward's brother-in-law, the son of the powerful Earl Godwin of Wessex. Godwin had supported Cnut, Harthacnut and Edward the Confessor during their reigns, and by the end of his life he was arguably more powerful than the King. Harold was a highly competent member of his father's entourage and also loyally supported Edward the Confessor, even against his own rebellious brothers, Swein of Mercia and Tostig of Northumbria, who were later both exiled. He married Edith, daughter of the Earl of Mercia, and widow of Gruffydd ap Llywelyn, the only native ruler to exercise power throughout Wales. He also had a famous mistress, Edith Swan Neck, and had five or six illegitimate children.

On the death of King Edward, Harold was named as his successor and approved by the King's council, the Witan. But this did not cut much ice with Scandinavian and Norman claimants to the throne. The lack of royal blood in Harold's veins was a serious weakness for which he was to pay dearly.

When Harold was crowned in 1066, the nation came under

immediate threat of invasion from Normandy and Norway. Defences against William of Normandy were prepared, but the first threat to materialize came from King Harald Hardrada of Norway. Hardrada was supported by Tostig, Harold Godwinson's younger brother, who had been dispossessed of his Northumbrian earldom. The Norwegian army landed in the north and defeated the earls of Mercia and Northumbria near York. They were resting at Stamford Bridge when the English army, led by Harold, appeared as if from nowhere and after a terrific struggle completely defeated the Norwegians, killing Tostig and Hardrada.

News then reached Harold that William of Normandy had landed at Pevensey and was laying waste to the countryside. Rather than waiting for reinforcements, Harold marched southwards to deal with the Normans. The two armies clashed at Senlac, near Hastings. The English held out all day but as the evening approached, a retreat by the Normans gave the tiring English a hope of outright victory, and they broke their shield wall to pursue the Normans. Either by design or strength of will, the Normans rallied, routing the English and killing Harold and his brothers. An English warrior depicted in the Bayeux Tapestry as being shot through the eye with an arrow, may or may not be Harold.

After the Battle of Hastings, the English held London against William for a while, but eventually made the decision to surrender to a strong king rather than fight to put a weak one on the throne, the only other contender (as all of Harold's brothers had been killed) being Edgar the Atheling, Edmund Ironside's grandson, who was still a young boy. Perhaps the success of King Cnut's reign reduced their fears of submitting to another foreign king.

THE NORMANS

ॐ

The Normans were Vikings (Northmen) who settled in France from the ninth century onwards. The French king accepted their control of Normandy in 911 and gave them the title of Dukes of Normandy. Gradually they became integrated with the French, and practised a particularly ruthless form of feudalism that enabled them to turn out well-equipped, well-trained and fearless warriors. They conquered England and parts of Scotland, Ireland, and Sicily, and ran the Christian kingdom in the Holy Land. The Normans' castles and architecture formed a lasting legacy in England, as did the contribution of French words to the English language.

WILLIAM I
Reigned 1066–1087

The legacy of William the Conqueror is debated. Was he the man who destroyed Anglo-Saxon England? Or did he lay the foundation for the glorious future of the nation? On the one hand, William eradicated the English aristocracy, replacing it with the feudal system, with the hated French as powerful barons, thereby creating a Britain divided by class. On the other hand, the Norman Conquest was responsible for merging the practicality of the Anglo-Saxons with the flair of the French, creating a hybrid race and language that proved stronger and more adaptable as a result. By the end of William's reign virtually every major landlord was French, every leading clergyman was foreign, and the English language had been replaced with French and Latin.

William was born in 1027/8 in Falaise Castle, Normandy, the illegitimate son of Robert, Duke of Normandy, and a tanner's daughter. He succeeded to the Dukedom as a child in 1035 and conquered Maine (in northern France) in 1063. In 1066 he claimed the throne of England on the death of Edward the Confessor. His claim was very weak but he said it had been offered to him by Edward and that Edward's 'official' successor, Harold Godwinson, had vowed to support it (this was disputed by Harold). William received the support of the Pope and gathered a huge fleet full of freebooters, willing to risk all for the spoils of war. His victory over King Harold at the Battle of Hastings on 14 October 1066 marks one of the most important dates in the course of English history.

William's coronation on Christmas Day 1066 at Westminster Abbey was a disaster, as Norman troops ran riot after mistaking sounds of acclamation coming from within the abbey for an English rebellion. This set the tone for much of his early reign, as William dealt with continued resistance ruthlessly. The Saxon leader Hereward the Wake was causing trouble in East Anglia; Edgar the Atheling and the earls of Mercia and Northumbria, supported by the Danes, led a rebellion in the north; and there were uprisings in the Midlands. In response, William adopted a scorched-earth policy, which included genocide and the salting of the land in the infamous 'Harrying of the North'. The consequence was mass starvation, and the north took decades to recover. The creation of the royal forests – swathes of land that were cleared of Saxon villages and reserved for the sole use of the King and his nobles – was also deeply resented.

However, William maintained a well-ordered, strong kingdom in which crime was contained. The efficiency of Norman bureaucracy is shown by the creation of the Domesday Book, a comprehensive survey of who owned what in England, which was completed in 1086, shortly before William's death in Rouen from war wounds in 1087. William married Matilda of Flanders and had ten children. Remarkably for this time, he seems to have remained faithful to his wife.

WILLIAM II
Reigned 1087–1100

William II was the fifth child and third son of William the Conqueror, and was born in around 1056 in Normandy. His fair hair and ruddy complexion earned him the nickname 'Rufus' (meaning 'red'). He was a rather flamboyant figure, with 'effeminate' long hair and extravagant clothes, and is said to have led a dissolute life. He never married and was not linked with any women, which in an age when the succession was the most important matter of state is quite startling and has led to suggestions that he was gay.

However, he was a strong warrior who conquered all those he faced in battle, although he was more generous and less ruthless than his father. He was able to consolidate the Norman rule over England and to protect and extend the Normandy homelands, which had been given to his older brother, Robert. The two brothers intrigued and fought against each other constantly until 1096, when Robert leased Normandy to William in exchange for money, which Robert needed in order to join the First Crusade.

William may have been an excellent king, but he was given an exceedingly bad write-up by the monks who recorded history. This is not surprising, given that throughout his reign he did much to antagonize the Church. He delayed appointing church leaders, so that he could enjoy their incomes, and fought with Rome over whether the King or the Pope had the final say when it came to church appointments. He eventually drove the saintly Archbishop of Canterbury, Anselm, into exile.

There has been much speculation about William's mysterious death, when he was struck by an arrow while hunting in the New Forest. William's younger brother, Henry, was a member of the hunting party that day and had much to gain from his brother's death.

HENRY I
Reigned 1100–1135

Born in 1068 in Selby, Yorkshire, Henry was the youngest and only English-born son of William the Conqueror. Although his father denied him the kingdom he craved, Henry did inherit his ruthless determination. Neither of his older brothers, Robert and William, trusted him and they agreed that Henry would inherit neither Normandy nor England upon their deaths. However, in 1100, Henry's opportunity came. Robert was away on the First Crusade when William II was killed in a 'hunting accident' in the New Forest. Henry was nearby and abandoned his brother's corpse to gallop to the capital, Winchester, to secure the treasury and the throne for himself. Three days later, he was crowned.

Henry was clever, educated and a master diplomat. He used his English birth, along with generous gifts and bribes, to gain support from the English, who were still smarting from the Norman Conquest. He married Matilda, who was not only the great-granddaughter of Edmund Ironside but also the daughter of Malcolm III of Scotland, and their son William was given the Anglo-Saxon title of Atheling. One source gives Henry and Matilda the English nicknames 'Gaffer Goodrich' and 'Goody Maud'. In reality, though, Henry was a Norman through and through.

Within six years of being crowned, Henry had defeated Robert in Normandy and reunited the two dominions. Robert was imprisoned for twenty-six years, eventually dying in Cardiff Castle. He was said to have been blinded after a failed escape attempt.

Much of the rest of his reign was spent protecting Normandy from threats and rebellions, many focusing on Robert's son, who had been spared the fate of his father. Desperately short of money,

Henry developed the English legal system and bureaucracy in order to fund his government, thereby limiting the independence of the rapacious Norman aristocracy. Among the King's achievements, therefore, are the foundations of the English common law system and the development of a powerful treasury, or Exchequer (the name coming from the chequerboard table Henry used as an abacus when agreeing accounts with his subjects).

Henry had four legitimate children with Matilda, none with his second wife, Adeliza, and an astonishing twenty-five or more illegitimate offspring. But in 1120 hopes for a return to legitimate English rule under the Atheling, William, were dashed when he and his younger brother Richard were drowned in the 'White Ship', when it went down off the Normandy coast. They were Henry's only legitimate sons, so he was forced to appoint his daughter Matilda as his heir. Henry died in 1135 of a 'surfeit of Lamphreys' (similar to eels).

STEPHEN
Reigned 1135–1154

Stephen was a nephew of Henry I. He was born in around 1097 at Blois in France. His older brother succeeded as Count of Blois, while Stephen and his brother Henry (later Bishop of Winchester) sought their fortune with the Normans and were made hugely wealthy with the King's support. The heir to Henry I's throne was his daughter Matilda who, when Henry died in 1135, was married to Geoffrey, Count of Anjou. The Normans were not prepared to have a queen as their monarch, and certainly not one who was married to one of their Angevin enemies, so Stephen saw his chance to make a bid for the throne. Within weeks of his uncle's death, he had succeeded.

Stephen was 'a mild man who was soft and good', qualities which explain both his popularity and the fact that his reign was so chaotic. Things started off well, but he was soon faced with civil war, when Matilda invaded England in 1139, while her husband attacked Normandy. This period is known as the Anarchy – the 'nineteen long winters' of strife during which the local lords were virtually unrestrained by the warring powers. When his forces captured Matilda a more ruthless king would have finished the civil war with a brutal murder; instead Matilda escaped, and in 1141 the tables were turned when Stephen was himself captured after the Battle of Lincoln. Matilda took the throne, the first English reigning queen, though she styled herself 'Lady of the English'.

Preparations were put in place for a glorious coronation, but Stephen's redoubtable wife, also called Matilda (of Boulogne), rallied his supporters and advanced on London. Londoners turned against the haughty, unpopular Queen and 'like thronging swarms from beehives' forced her to flee. Her principal supporter, Robert of Gloucester, an illegitimate son of Henry I, was captured and Matilda was forced to free Stephen in an exchange of prisoners.

Stephen regained the initiative and the throne, and captured Matilda at Oxford Castle in 1142, but she escaped yet again, climbing down the castle walls and fleeing across the frozen river. Matilda's son Henry gathered together a small army of mercenaries to invade England, but ran out of money to pay his soldiers. Unbelievably, Stephen gave Henry the money he needed, while rallying support for his own son, Eustace, as heir. But the death of Eustace and Henry's control of Normandy, which had been taken by his father in 1144, made Stephen's position increasingly difficult. Faced with an invasion by Henry, Stephen agreed that on his death Henry would take the throne, while Stephen's youngest son, William, would inherit all his father's lands but renounce his own claim. The civilized agreement was some reward for Stephen's kindness, and the Anarchy was at an end.

Stephen and his wife had five children, and he had a further five illegitimate children.

THE PLANTAGENETS

❧

A s Henry I had no surviving sons the crown was disputed
between his nephew, Stephen, and his daughter, Matilda. She
married Geoffrey the Handsome of the French district of Anjou,
which bordered Normandy. He was also nicknamed after the broom
blossom or 'plante genêt' as it was known in French, a yellow sprig
of which he wore in his hat. The marriage was supposed to seal
peace between Normandy and Anjou, but the accession of Stephen
led to war. When Henry II, son of Geoffrey and Matilda, ascended
the English throne, it meant that England was now part of an
Angevin or Plantagenet empire rather than a Norman one.

HENRY II
Reigned 1154–1189

Henry II can be ranked as one of the greatest kings of England, and at the height of his power he controlled most of Britain and much of France. He was educated, but straightforward, and had no love of ostentation. He was a formidable general and a vigorous leader, with a terrible temper and an unrestrained sexual appetite. Henry had up to twelve illegitimate children by more than four mistresses, to add to the eight children he had with his wife, Eleanor of Aquitaine.

He was born in 1133 at Le Mans in France, the son of Geoffrey, the Count of Anjou, and Empress Matilda. When his father died in 1151, he succeeded him as Count of Anjou, with dominion over the French regions of Touraine, Anjou, Maine and Normandy. In 1152 he pulled off a spectacular marriage to the sublime Eleanor of Aquitaine, who had just divorced the King of France, Louis VII, which brought Poitou and Gascony under his control. King Louis was horrified by the loss of such rich provinces to a rival and declared war. He was easily defeated by Henry, who then turned his attention to England. In 1153 he boldly crossed the Channel. War was averted by the fortuitous death of King Stephen's heir and it was agreed that Henry would succeed. He was crowned in 1154 and moved quickly to consolidate and expand his new kingdom. He re-established control over Northumbria, garrisoned Edinburgh, invaded Wales, got the Pope's permission to invade Ireland and gained control of Brittany.

He oversaw his vast empire by ceaseless travel. He built on the Anglo-Saxon local government system to maintain central control while he was away, while at the same time reducing the independence of the mighty barons. He made them demolish unauthorized castles and ended the hereditary appointment of law officers. He continued with the reforms of Henry I, further developing the English common law system, including the establishment of trial by jury, and ending the age-old systems of trial by combat or ordeal.

But these substantial achievements were diminished by the events of his later years. His first major setback occurred when Thomas Becket, a friend whom Henry had elevated to the position of Archbishop of Canterbury, stubbornly took the Pope's side in disputes concerning the power of the Church. In 1170 a furious Henry demanded, 'Will no one rid me of this turbulent priest?' This was interpreted as a command, and Becket was brutally assassinated by four knights on the steps of Canterbury Cathedral. In penance, Henry walked barefoot to the site of the murder while being scourged by the clergy. Becket was later canonized.

Even more distressing was the behaviour of three of his four sons, Henry, Richard and Geoffrey. They demanded independent domains and eventually, egged on by their mother, Eleanor, who by this time was estranged from her promiscuous husband, they rebelled in 1173. Henry defeated them and Eleanor was imprisoned.

Henry and Geoffrey died, leaving Richard and Henry II's youngest and favourite son, John, in line to inherit the empire. But not satisfied with this, Richard sought the support of the new King of France, Philip II. By this time Henry was suffering from ill health and he was forced to make peace. He died just a few days later, a broken man, having heard that his beloved John had also been part of the conspiracy against him.

RICHARD I
Reigned 1189–1199

Richard the Lionheart was the epitome of the warrior king. He was tall and handsome, a great general and a cultured product of the age of chivalry. Although he has a reputation as a great king, he spent only a few months of his reign in England and spoke very little English.

He was born at Beaumont Palace in Oxford in 1157, the second son of Henry II and Eleanor of Aquitaine to reach adulthood. He spent his early years in his mother's duchy, and inherited it in 1172. Richard first rebelled against his father at the age of sixteen and a decade of strife broke out between them. After the death of Richard's older brother Henry, the heir to the throne of England, Richard defeated his father, who died soon after.

Richard immediately went to England to prepare for his coronation and raise money for the Third Crusade, with the aim of taking back the Holy city of Jerusalem from the Muslim leader Saladin and the Saracens. He left his grandmother Matilda in charge in Normandy, and his mother, Eleanor, in England. The Third Crusade failed to recapture Jerusalem, but Richard did manage to conquer Cyprus and Acre and proved a worthy rival to the great Saladin. He was ruthless in victory: after the siege of Acre, Richard had 2,700 Muslim prisoners of war slaughtered.

Meanwhile, in England, trouble was brewing due to the arrogance of Richard's deputy, William Longchamp, and the intrigues of Richard's younger brother John, who was rallying support for his own cause, and Philip II of France, who was preparing to invade Normandy. So, in 1192, Richard hastily concluded peace with Saladin and set off for home. But on the way he was captured by

Leopold of Austria and sold to the Holy Roman Emperor. A huge ransom was demanded, despite the Pope excommunicating the captors. The sum was eventually raised, through heavy taxation of his English subjects, and although both John and Philip II offered the captors money to keep Richard imprisoned, he was released and returned to England in 1194 to be triumphantly recrowned. He left again almost immediately, to win back territories from the French. He succeeded in this, but in 1199 he was wounded in the arm by an arrow at the siege of Chalus and died of an infection. He had no children by his wife, Berengaria of Navarre, leaving his brother John as his successor. He had two illegitimate children.

KING JOHN
Reigned 1199–1216

'Foul as it is, Hell itself is defiled by the fouler presence of John,' wrote a thirteenth-century monk. John was a deeply unpopular monarch, nicknamed 'Lackland' and 'Softsword', whose disastrous reign lost England most of the French territories his father and brother had defended so fiercely and also ended with civil war.

John was born in 1166 at Beaumont Palace in Oxford, the youngest son of the formidable Henry II and Eleanor of Aquitaine. Attempts to find the young prince lands to rule led to war with his brother Richard over Aquitaine, failure as Lord of Ireland and eventually to the betrayal of his own father. Later, Prince John conspired to seize the throne from Richard, and although his attempts failed, John finally became king when Richard died in 1199.

King John divorced his childless first wife and married Isabella of Angoulême, a marriage designed to knit his French territories together. Unfortunately, she was already betrothed to a French nobleman, Hugh de Lusignan. Outraged, Hugh appealed to King Philip II of France. When John ignored a summons to appear before him, Philip declared that John's French lands were forfeit. In the war that followed, John had some early success, capturing the Lusignans and his own nephew Arthur of Brittany, who was imprisoned and murdered. But the murder lost John the valuable support of many French nobles and he was forced to abandon his campaign and flee to England, although an expedition to Poitou in 1206 saved Aquitaine for the English Crown.

John spent the next eight years amassing money to renew his campaign to win back his French territories, antagonizing the English with his rapacious demands and heavy taxation. When John disputed Pope Innocent III's choice of Stephen Langton as Archbishop of Canterbury, the Pope banned all church services and Christian burials in England and John was excommunicated in 1209. In 1212 the Pope declared him deposed. Facing a revolt from his disgruntled barons and an attack by Philip II, John was forced to reconcile with the Pope, whom he acknowledged as England's overlord.

In 1214 John launched his big attack to win back his French lands. With the Pope's help, he orchestrated a coalition with Otto IV of Germany and Count Ferrand of Flanders, but it was decisively defeated at the Battle of Bouvines. This was a disaster. In losing Brittany, Normandy, Maine, Anjou and Touraine, John had undone one hundred years of successful empire-building. With his position so greatly weakened, the rebellious barons forced the King to sign the Magna Carta in 1215 at Runnymede, an important document that symbolized the principle that the King was not above the law and that his subjects had the right to due process of law and were protected from arbitrary arrest.

But John had no intention of keeping to its terms and soon persuaded the Pope to revoke it, leading to civil war. The barons gave their support to Philip II's son, Louis, who landed in Britain and by May 1216 had captured Winchester and London. King John died later that same year, having over-indulged in peaches and new cider, leaving his diminished, threatened kingdom to his nine-year-old son, Henry. John had five children with Isabella and twelve illegitimate children.

HENRY III
Reigned 1216–1272

Henry was a God-fearing, family-loving man, but although his reign was a long one, he was a naive and weak king. His failures as a soldier and diplomat meant that he did not recover the French territories lost by his father, and his reputation was further damaged by his preference for foreign advisors and his outrageous financial demands.

Henry was born at Winchester Castle in 1207 and was nine years old when his father, John, died in 1216. He was crowned in Gloucester because London and Winchester were under the control of Prince Louis of France, and with his mother's circlet because the Crown Jewels had been lost in the Wash. His position seemed precarious, but the honesty and commitment of his regent, William

Marshal, saved him from the French, and Louis withdrew in 1217. The Magna Carta was reissued that same year, and by the time Marshal died in 1219, the country was ruled by a committee of barons led by Hubert de Burgh.

Henry came of age in 1227 and began his personal rule, ending baronial control and replacing them with hated foreign advisors. He made matters worse by raising taxes to pay for a campaign to recapture the French territories, an attempt to buy the kingdom of Sicily for his son and his plans to rebuild Westminster Abbey and the Tower of London. Only his architectural adventures were successful, especially at Westminster, where his work remains a physical embodiment of his conception of kingship, but he was left with no new territories and a ruined country.

The barons, led by Henry's brother-in-law Simon de Montfort, revolted and forced the King to accept the Provisions of Oxford in 1258, which limited his power and reintroduced a baronial governing council. For the first time, the Crown was forced to recognize the rights of Parliament, which was to meet three times a year. The King turned to the Pope for help and civil war broke out once again.

De Montfort captured Henry and his son Edward at the Battle of Lewes in 1264, and effectively took over the kingdom. In 1265 he called Europe's first elected parliament, with elected representatives from both the major towns and the counties. Unluckily for de Montfort, however, Prince Edward had escaped his imprisonment and formed an army, and de Montfort was defeated and killed at the Battle of Evesham in 1265. Although Henry lived for another seven years after regaining his throne, his much more effective son was in de facto control of the country, leaving Henry free to pursue his great passion – patronage of the arts – until his death in 1272.

EDWARD I
Reigned 1272–1307

Edward was born in 1239 at Westminster. Known as 'Longshanks' (he was 6ft 2in) and 'the Lawgiver', he was the nearest thing to a proper English king since Harold II. He even spoke English, albeit with a lisp. By the time he came to the throne in 1272, he had already proved himself to be a formidable and determined military leader, having rescued his father, Henry III, and defeated the rebel Simon de Montfort at the Battle of Evesham in 1265. When Henry died, Edward was on a crusade with his wife, Eleanor of Castile, who accompanied him on most of his military campaigns, and so he was not crowned until two years later. The transition arrangements, with the new King absent overseas, were remarkably successful and proved a model for future stable successions.

Edward undertook a massive reform of the legal system in an effort to stamp out corruption among royal officials, codifying many existing laws in the 1275 Statute of Westminster, and he further developed the parliamentary format set up by Simon de Montfort. However, the motive for most of his reforms was financial. He also began an attack on Jews who had settled in England after the Norman Conquest and the practice of usury (money-lending at high rates of interest). In 1275 he issued a decree restricting Jewish business activities and made Jews wear a yellow badge. In 1279 he arrested all heads of Jewish families and had 300 of them executed, and in 1290, following riots, he expelled all Jews and confiscated their property.

Edward's main military policy during his reign was to assert his overlordship of the British Isles, turning his attention to Scotland and Wales, as he held only Gascony and the Channel Islands in France. His first target was Wales: Llywelyn ap Gruffydd, Prince of Wales, refused to pay homage to the new King, and after being defeated and pardoned, he revolted again in 1282. Edward responded with an overwhelming display of power. He ringed Snowdonia with a circle of tremendous fortresses, known as the Ring of Iron, and the native kingdoms were dismembered and integrated into the English system of counties. Edward's son, the future Edward II, became the first English Prince of Wales, and for the first time in its history Wales was no longer independent of its English neighbour.

When Alexander III of Scotland died in 1286, Edward asserted his right as overlord to choose his successor, giving his support to John Balliol rather than the more powerful Robert the Bruce in an attempt to subjugate the Scots. Unhappy with this situation, the Scots allied themselves with Philip IV of France, who had by this time seized Gascony. In 1296 Edward led a large army northwards and forced the Scots to surrender, seizing the Stone of Scone, the symbol of the Scottish monarchy. But the Scottish problem was by no means settled, and Edward suffered reverses at the hands of William Wallace and others. Wallace was eventually captured and executed in 1305, but the troubles in Scotland and emerging problems in France darkened Edward's later years. He died in 1307, en route to do battle with the new King of Scotland, Robert the Bruce.

EDWARD II
Reigned 1307–1327

Edward was born in 1284 at Caernarvon and was the first English Prince of Wales, a title his father bestowed on him in infancy, although the story of his presentation as a newborn to the people of Wales when they demanded a 'Prince who spoke no English' is a fabrication. Outwardly, he was the very vision of a king – tall, fair-haired and handsome – but he was not cut out for the responsibility. He was frivolous and flamboyant, shunning military campaigning in preference to the amusements of his court and hard physical labour alongside his peasants. His one foray north ended disastrously when he was beaten at Bannockburn in 1314 by a badly outnumbered Scottish army led by Robert the Bruce, which effectively ended English hopes of controlling Scotland.

Edward lavished money and power on his favourites at court, making some of the barons not only jealous but hot for revenge. They murdered Piers Gaveston, the King's great favourite, and gained control of the government. Determined on revenge, Edward regained power with the help of a couple of his supporters, Hugh le Despenser and his son, and executed two dozen nobles and exiled others. Back in charge, Edward and the Despensers ruled with scant regard for law and diplomacy and soon became hated.

Edward sent his wife, Isabella, known as 'the she-wolf of France', on a diplomatic mission back to France, where opponents of the King and the Despensers had gathered. Isabella – perhaps in revenge for Edward's humiliating preference for male companions – began an affair with Roger Mortimer, one of the exiled nobles and a sworn enemy of the Despensers. The couple plotted to overthrow the King and put his son, Prince Edward, on the throne. Having raised an army, they invaded in 1326 and England fell under their control.

Edward was imprisoned by Mortimer in 1327 and was forced to abdicate in favour of his son. Having been humiliated and tortured, he was then horribly murdered, on the orders of Mortimer, by the insertion of a red-hot poker through a horn tube into his rectum, a method designed to leave no external marks of violence.

EDWARD III
Reigned 1327–1377

For the most part, the reign of Edward III was a triumph of warfare. At one time, he held the kings of Scotland and France captive and had restored the English position in both countries. But he suffered reverses as he aged – and ultimately, what he won by the sword, he lost by the sword. Essentially, he outlived his own victories.

Edward was crowned aged fourteen in 1327, after the murder of his father. Three years later he avenged his father by arresting and executing his mother's lover, Roger Mortimer, who was acting as regent. His mother, Isabella of France, was exiled to Castle Rising in Norfolk.

Now free to rule as he saw fit, Edward sought to revoke Scottish independence by overthrowing the Scottish King David II and giving his support to rival claimant Edward Balliol. He met with some considerable initial success, culminating in the defeat of the Scots at Halidon Hill in 1333, but Balliol's position was weak and he was deposed in 1336. In 1346 David II invaded England but was defeated by the Archbishop of York, William la Zouche, at Neville's Cross and imprisoned.

Edward gained the support of his nobles by offering them the opportunity to enrich themselves with loot from his series of campaigns in France. With the death of Charles IV of France in 1324, the direct line of the Capetian dynasty had come to an end. Edward had enough of a claim to the throne, through his mother, to justify war and in 1337 he felt ready to declare his intentions, thus beginning the long-drawn-out conflict that would be known as the Hundred Years War. The sea battle of Sluys in 1340 destroyed the French navy, and the English had a decisive victory at the Battle of Crécy in 1346, in which the flower of the French knighthood was seen off by the English longbowmen, marking the end of the so-called 'Age of Chivalry'. The arrival of the Black Death of 1348, which killed at least one third of Europeans, led to a short truce, but war soon resumed. In 1356 Edward's son, the Black Prince, defeated the French at Poitiers and the French King, Jean II, was captured. However, the Black Prince fell ill, Edward's wife, Queen Philippa, died, and Edward descended into senility comforted by an unpopular mistress, Alice Perrers. He had thirteen children by Philippa and three illegitimate children by Alice. The King's third son, John of Gaunt, took over and a new French king reversed Edward's victories. The years of glory faded from memory, and by 1375 all that was left of the French empire was Calais, Bordeaux and Bayonne.

RICHARD II
Reigned 1377–1399

Richard was born in 1367 at Bordeaux, the son of the Black Prince, the eldest son of Edward III. He was crowned at the age of ten, and the country was controlled by his uncle, John of Gaunt, the Duke of Lancaster.

Richard's finest hour came in June 1381, when at the age of fourteen he ended the Peasants' Revolt. Serfs from Essex and Kent, led by Wat Tyler and John Ball, took control of London to protest against the poll tax. With the army divided between Scotland and France, the peasants besieged the Tower of London and seized and executed the Chancellor and Treasurer of England, amongst others. Negotiations with the King were indecisive until the final meeting took place at Smithfield. Wat Tyler, supported by 30,000 peasants, rode towards the King's small party to demand the end of serfdom, the abolition of the Lords, the reform of the Commons and changes to the Church. A dispute arose and Tyler was stabbed by the Lord Mayor of London, at which point the peasants were poised to attack. The young King defused a very dangerous situation by riding forward and promising to be the peasants' leader. The peasants dispersed. Back in control, King Richard reneged on his promise and is reported to have said, 'Serfs, you are, and serfs you will remain, only incomparably viler than hitherto.'

Richard's arrogance, bad temper and intolerance of criticism led to a fraught relationship with his barons, and he found it hard to break free of their control as he approached the age of majority. In 1388 a group of magnates that included Richard's cousin Henry Bolingbroke, John of Gaunt's son, formed a council called the Lords Appellant and had many of Richard's supporters executed.

The King came of age in 1389, and there followed a period of peace during which Richard gradually rebuilt his power base. As a lover of fashion, ostentatious display and architecture, he set up a magnificent household and completed Henry III's Westminster Abbey. But revenge was burning in his heart, and he built up a private army recruited from Wales, Ireland and Chester. In 1397 he struck, executing or banishing his leading opponents, including Henry Bolingbroke, who was exiled for ten years.

On the death of John of Gaunt in 1399, Richard seized all of Bolingbroke's land and increased his exile to life. But Bolingbroke took advantage of Richard's absence on a campaign in Ireland and invaded the country with a small force, claiming, at first, that he had only come to reclaim his rightful inheritance. Richard's support drained away, and he was arrested, imprisoned in the Tower and forced to abdicate. He was then sent to Pontefract Castle, where he was almost certainly murdered in early 1400.

LANCASTER
AND YORK

&

The murder of Richard II ended the direct Plantagenet line. The throne was taken by Henry IV who was the son of Edward III's third surviving son, John of Gaunt, Duke of Lancaster. So those descended from this line are called Lancastrians. However, the incapacity of Henry VI brought civil war in which the descendants of Edward III's fourth son, Edmund, Duke of York, also claimed the throne (hence their name, the Yorkists). Being descended from the fourth son is inferior to being descended from the third, so the Yorkists made their claim on the basis of also being descended from Edward III's second son, Lionel, Duke of Clarence, through his great-granddaughter Anne Mortimer. It was Anne's son, Richard, Duke of York, who eventually started the bloody Wars of the Roses between the two branches of the Plantagenet family. The red rose symbolized Lancaster and the white rose York, although these were not used on the rival badges at the time.

HENRY IV
Reigned 1399–1413

H enry was born at Bolingbroke Castle, Lincolnshire, in 1367, the grandson of Edward III. Although he participated in the 1388 Lords Appellant's rebellion against his cousin King Richard II, he was initially forgiven. He was a great warrior and completed his military training fighting with the Teutonic Knights in Lithuania and on the long journey to Jerusalem. On returning to England, he was forced into exile by Richard in 1398, and, on the death of his father, John of Gaunt, in 1399 he was disinherited. But he returned to England with a small armed force and power fell into his lap. The tyrannical Richard was imprisoned and persuaded to abdicate, and Henry was declared king. He immediately faced rebellions from Richard's supporters, so Henry probably had him murdered, an act which was to be a terrible burden on his conscience for the rest of his life.

In 1400 Henry was faced with a rebellion in Wales, when Owain Glyn Dwr declared himself Prince of Wales, supported by Edmund Mortimer and the charismatic Henry 'Hotspur' Percy, the Earl of Northumberland's son. Mortimer had previously supported Henry IV despite having a better claim to the throne himself, but Henry was slow to ransom him when he was captured by Owain. So Mortimer decided to make his own claim to the throne in conjunction with Owain. In addition, the powerful Northumberland Percy family, who had done sterling work for Richard and Henry against the Scots, Welsh and French, felt unrewarded by Henry and switched their support to Mortimer and the rebel Welsh leader. The plan was for Owain to take Wales, Mortimer England and to leave Northumberland for the Percy family.

This was a desperate threat to Henry, so in 1403 he hastened to Shrewsbury to confront Henry Hotspur. It was a terrible battle, with a great number of casualties falling in particular to the archers. Both Henry's son, the future Henry V, and Hotspur were struck in the face by arrows, but Hotspur was pierced through the brain and he died, giving the victory to Henry.

The threat from the north remained until Henry defeated the Earl of Northumberland and executed the Archbishop of York, who had sided with the Percys. With the end of the Welsh rebellion in 1409, Henry's regime was secure and the financial difficulties that had plagued his early years diminished, but the execution of the Archbishop was another burden on his conscience. His final years were affected by a variety of unknown illnesses, which may have been at least partially psychosomatic, although some said he had been poisoned by his second wife, Joan of Navarre, who was accused of being a witch, and others claimed he was a leper. In 1413 he fell ill in Westminster Abbey and died in the Jerusalem Chamber, fulfilling a prophesy that he would die in Jerusalem.

HENRY V
Reigned 1413–1422

Henry was one of our greatest warrior kings. It is a tragedy that he died so young and that his remarkable achievements came to nothing because of the ineffective reign of his only son, Henry VI. He was born at Monmouth Castle in 1386 or 1387, the son of Henry IV and his first wife, Mary de Bohun. When his father came to the throne, young Henry was made Prince of Wales. There is no real evidence that he spent his youth in dissipation, as depicted by Shakespeare. In fact, quite the contrary, he spent his early years fighting to keep hold of his principality. As a teenager, he was trusted with leading the right wing of his father's army against the heroic Harry Hotspur at the Battle of Shrewsbury in 1403, where he received a terrible facial wound which disfigured him for life.

As his father's health deteriorated, Henry took an increasing role in government. On succeeding to the throne in 1413, Henry survived an early coup attempt and began a policy of reconciliation, restoring titles and land to the heirs of those who had rebelled against his father. He founded new religious communities and helped bring to an end the schism in the Catholic Church (at one point there were three competing popes). He also promoted the English language, the first king since 1066 to use it in correspondence and government records.

Henry's main aim, however, was to win back the lost territories in France. In 1415 he nearly met with disaster at Agincourt, where the small English force was forced into battle against a vastly superior French army. But because of superb generalship, the skill of the English archers and the over-confidence of the French, Henry turned a potential disaster into a triumph. He followed up this success with methodical planning, and had soon reconquered Normandy, occasionally resorting to barbaric tactics, and gained the ascendancy in France. The French King, Charles VI, was forced to sign the Treaty of Troyes in 1420, which stated that Henry would inherit the throne upon his death, and Henry married Charles's daughter Catherine that same year. But Henry was not to fulfil his ambition to sit on the French throne, for he died on campaign in 1422, leaving the infant Henry VI to inherit the fruits of his success.

HENRY VI
Reigned 1422–1461; 1470–1471

King Henry VI was the polar opposite of his heroic father, Henry V. The Pope described him as 'a man more timorous than a woman, utterly devoid of wit and spirit'. He was very religious and generous of spirit, but he was not cut out for government.

He was born in 1421 at Windsor Castle and became king when his father died nine months later. He inherited the French throne less than eight weeks later, on the death of Charles VI, but this was hotly disputed by his uncle the Dauphin and his supporters. Henry's government was controlled by his uncles, the Dukes of Gloucester and Bedford, who did a fairly good job until the King came of age in 1437 and took control.

Unfortunately, Henry did not have the personality or consistency to rule wisely. The fortunes of the French had revived through the success of Joan of Arc in Orleans in 1429, and the Dauphin had been crowned Charles VII of France. Under Henry, loss of territory in France accelerated. He made matters worse by marrying Margaret of Anjou in 1445, for which he had to hand over Anjou and Maine to the French. By 1453 Normandy and Aquitaine had been lost, leaving only Calais in English hands – the entire life's work of Henry V was undone.

In 1453, Henry had his first mental breakdown and his cousin Richard, Duke of York, was made regent. Richard put the Earl of Somerset in the Tower, blaming him for the loss of lands in France. When the King recovered, Somerset was freed and Richard relieved of his regency. But fighting soon broke out between Richard, Duke of York, supported by the Earl of Warwick (the Yorkists), and the royal party, led by the Earl of Somerset and Queen Margaret, and supported by the Percys of Northumberland (the Lancastrians). This was the start of the thirty-year Wars of the Roses.

In the power struggle that followed, the Duke of York was close to seizing the throne on several occasions. He defeated and killed Somerset at the Battle of St Albans, and defeated the Queen's forces at Northampton in 1460, capturing the King. Henry was forced to make York his heir, despite the fact that he already had a son, Edward. But later that same year, York was killed when the two sides clashed at Wakefield and the Yorkist mantle passed to his charismatic son, Edward, Earl of March, who seized the throne in 1461, keeping Henry VI in the Tower of London. Edward ruled well for nine years, until he fell out with the Earl of Warwick, who made an alliance with King Louis of France and Margaret. Together they forced the unprepared Edward into exile and put Henry VI back on the throne as their puppet in 1470.

But Edward returned in 1471, killing Warwick at the Battle of Barnet and Henry's heir, Edward, at the Battle of Tewkesbury. Edward came to the conclusion that Henry's continued existence was dangerous and Henry was probably murdered in the Tower of London later that year, although it was announced that he died of grief.

EDWARD IV
Reigned 1461–1470; 1471–1483

E dward was born in Rouen in 1442, the son of Richard, Duke of York. He seized the throne from Henry VI in 1461, shortly after his father was killed in battle, and imprisoned Henry in the Tower of London.

He was a popular king. He was charming and handsome, and he had the common touch, remembering names and putting people at their ease. His reign might have been triumphant but for two major mistakes. The first was his marriage to Elizabeth Woodville. She was a widow whom Edward married in secret, seemingly because she would not submit to him despite 'gifts and menaces'. The marriage destroyed Edward's crucial relationship with the Earl of Warwick, who had been instrumental in putting Edward on the throne, as it ruined Warwick's plans for a French marriage. The proud Warwick switched his allegiance to the Lancastrians, made an alliance with the French King and restored Henry VI to the throne in 1470. Edward was forced into exile, although he recovered his throne in 1471 and had Henry murdered.

Edward's second mistake was his failure to support the Duke of Burgundy against the French. The Burgundian alliance was the mainstay of English foreign policy throughout the Hundred Years War and helped protect vital English trading interests in the Low Countries. In return, Edward received a pension from Louis XI of France, but strategically the subsequent defeat of Burgundy was deeply unpopular and dangerous to England's long-term interests.

Apart from these mistakes, Edward's management provided good solutions to problems in Wales, Scotland and France. He also governed the country firmly, so that the economy flourished and law and order improved, and his regime remained popular.

However, the Queen's numerous relatives, the Woodvilles, became very unpopular, particularly with the old nobility, and it is possible to blame the Woodville marriage for the collapse of the Yorkist dynasty. It caused the revolt of Warwick and arguably led to the execution of one of Edward's brothers, the Duke of Clarence, who was drowned, it is said, in a barrel of wine.

Edward suffered a notable decline in his later years, becoming corpulent and lacking the energy and enthusiasm that marked the early years of his reign. His brother Richard, Duke of Gloucester, blamed his decline and subsequent death in 1483 on the Woodvilles, who had made the court a riotous place of feasting, drunkenness and intrigue.

King Edward had ten children by Elizabeth Woodville and at least four illegitimate children by three different mothers. His favourite mistress was Jane Shore, wife of a City merchant.

EDWARD V
Reigned 1483

Edward was born in 1470 at Westminster, the son of Edward IV and Elizabeth Woodville. He was declared king on the death of his father in 1483, with his uncle Richard, Duke of Gloucester, as regent. The young King Edward V had been brought up by his mother's relatives, and the opening days of the new reign saw the Woodvilles attempt to exclude Richard from his position as Lord Protector. They set up their own ruling council and ordered an immediate coronation of the twelve-year-old king, who was still to arrive from Ludlow, his seat as Prince of Wales.

But Richard was warned by the loyal Lord Hastings that he faced what amounted to a coup, so he intercepted the young King on his way to London and arrested the Woodville leaders. The Queen and her younger son (also called Richard) sought sanctuary in Westminster Abbey, but other members of the Woodville clan were executed. Edward was taken to the Tower of London (which served as a royal palace as well as a prison) and was joined a short time later by his younger brother.

Richard called a meeting of the full Council of the Protectorate in the Tower, where he accused the astounded Lord Hastings of a treasonable conspiracy with the Woodvilles. Richard had Hastings executed immediately without trial. Plans for Edward's coronation were then put on hold, as Richard sought to have the King and his brother declared illegitimate, on the grounds that Edward IV had been contracted to marry another woman before marrying Elizabeth Woodville in secret. Parliament accepted this, declared Richard king and he was crowned on 6 July.

Nobody knows for sure what happened to the two boys, but they were never again seen outside the Tower. Were they murdered and if so at whose command? Richard clearly had the motive and the opportunity. Did he personally give the order? Or was it an overzealous supporter who took matters into his own hands? It is worth noting that the Duke of Buckingham and Henry Tudor both had claims to the throne and would also benefit from the death of the Princes. And if they could manage this while placing the blame on Richard, they would kill two birds with one stone. Whatever the case, the Princes simply vanished – no announcements, accusations or excuses were made. Most people blamed the obvious suspect. In 1674 bones of two young boys were found at the foot of a staircase in the Tower and were reburied in Westminster Abbey as the remains of the Princes in the Tower, but the truth remains elusive.

RICHARD III
Reigned 1483–1485

Richard's life falls into two halves: the first part when he served his brother King Edward IV and his country with loyalty and distinction, and the second part when as Protector and King he displayed a remarkable capacity for decisive and ruthless action.

He was born in 1452 at Fotheringay Castle, Northamptonshire. He finished his education in the home of the Earl of Warwick, where he met Anne Neville, who would later be his queen. By the age of seventeen Richard was a leading figure in the civil war and commanded wings of Edward's army at the crucial battles of Barnet and Tewkesbury, where Warwick and the Lancastrian forces were resoundingly defeated.

Richard was given responsibility for the north, where he ruled with diligence and fairness. He ended the Scottish threat, recaptured Berwick and occupied Edinburgh, and gave his brother's regime some much-needed military success. But he was not charismatic like his brother. He preferred to stay out of London to avoid the debauchery and intrigue of the London court.

When his brother died in April 1483, Richard was in a very difficult position. The young Edward V had been brought up by the Woodvilles, whom Richard blamed for the ill health and early death of the King. If they gained control, the consequences for Richard were grave. So he took decisive action, executing various members of the Woodville clan and keeping the young King and his brother in the Tower while he sought to have them declared illegitimate. He was successful in this, and was crowned in July 1483. The fate of the two boys remains unknown, but it is likely that they were murdered in the Tower that same year, possibly at Richard's behest.

Was the failure of Richard's reign caused by public revulsion at the Princes' murders, or was his real failure that he could not command the loyalty of those around him? His first year saw his betrayal by his main supporter, the Duke of Buckingham, who joined an alliance composed of the Woodvilles and Henry Tudor, a rival claimant to the throne. Buckingham was executed. Richard was also betrayed by Lord Stanley and the Earl of Northumberland at the Battle of Bosworth in 1485, and bravely went to his death in a last 'do or die' charge aimed at killing Henry Tudor. His crucial mistake had been to narrow his power base and rely on his old northern followers, thus alienating key nobles.

Richard had fathered up to seven illegitimate offspring before he married Anne Neville, but his one legitimate son had recently died aged nine, leaving the way clear for Henry Tudor to inherit the throne.

In 2012 there was much excitement among historians, as his purported remains were discovered during the excavation of a car park in Leicester. After scientific analysis of the skeleton, which revealed Richard did have a deformed spine, he was given a royal funeral and reburied at Leicester Cathedral in 2015.

THE TUDORS

෴

The Wars of the Roses killed off many of the leading contenders for the throne. The death of Edward of Lancaster, the son of Henry VI, made Henry Tudor the prominent Lancastrian claimant to the throne, through his mother's side – even though this Beaufort ancestry (being originally illegitimate) in fact gave him no legal claim at all. His father, Edmund Tudor, was descended from the Welsh prince Rhys ap Gruffudd. Henry's marriage to Elizabeth of York united the Yorkist and Lancastrian lines in the form of their son, Henry VIII. The massacre of aristocrats that took place in the Wars of the Roses and in the subsequent executions ordered by Henry VII and VIII is one of the factors that explains why the medieval age is deemed to have ended with the coming of the Tudors.

HENRY VII
Reigned 1485–1509

Henry Tudor had at best a very weak claim to the throne, but he was propelled to the top of the Lancastrian leader board by the deaths of Henry VI and his son. The subsequent deaths of Edward IV, the Duke of Clarence, the Princes in the Tower and the Duke of Buckingham killed off most of the leading Yorkist claimants, and in a short space of time turned Henry from an obscure Welsh noble to the main contender for the throne.

Henry was born in 1457 at Pembroke Castle, Wales. His mother, Margaret Beaufort, was a formidable woman who was descended from Edward III via an illegitimate son of John of Gaunt. On the Tudor side, Henry was descended from Catherine of Valois, Henry V's widow, who had secretly married a Welsh courtier, Owen Tudor.

Henry was forced into exile in Brittany when he was fourteen years old, and he spent the next fourteen years abroad, fathering one illegitimate child while he was there. Attempts to extradite him intensified under Richard III, but Henry escaped and fled to France, where he gained the support of the French King. In 1485, with a largely French army, Henry made the momentous decision to risk everything and try for the crown. He landed at Milford Haven, where his army was augmented by Welsh volunteers keen to see a Tudor on the throne of England. His success at the subsequent Battle of Bosworth was largely a matter of luck and the betrayal of Richard by leading supporters.

After he was proclaimed king, he fulfilled earlier promises and married Edward IV's daughter, Elizabeth of York, in order to unite the Lancastrian and Yorkist families. They had eight children together. Although the marriage is often cited as ending the Wars of the Roses, there was still much unrest, and Henry faced rebellions led by two imposters, Lambert Simnel and Perkin Warbeck, who pretended to be the Earl of Warwick and Richard of York (the younger of the Princes in the Tower). He also faced threats from the Yorkist claimant to the throne, John de la Pole, Earl of Lincoln (Edward IV and Richard III's nephew), as well as a Cornish rebellion that reached as far as London.

Henry was a shrewd ruler. He kept the nobility under control with heavy fines, so that fear of debt kept them compliant. He set up the Star Chamber, a small group of advisors which acted as a royal court and was able to act swiftly to protect the King's interests. Foreign relations were vastly improved, with commercial treaties being signed with Spain, Portugal, Denmark and the Netherlands. He was accused of avarice, over-taxing his subjects and hoarding his money, but this ensured a full treasury to hand over to his heir on his death in 1509.

HENRY VIII
Reigned 1509–1547

Henry VIII is arguably Britain's most famous monarch, but for all the wrong reasons. He was every inch a king, a man who knew how to command and expected to be obeyed. He combined his regal attributes with an egotism that did not shy away from transforming the entire country so that he got his own way.

He was born in 1491 at Greenwich Palace, the second son of Henry VII and Elizabeth of York. He was very well educated, being fluent in French, Spanish and Latin. He was interested in theology, music and poetry and had a passion for physical activity, including jousting, hunting, dancing and tennis. He was tall, athletic, handsome and charismatic.

Henry's reign began with wild optimism. The young, vital King's court was the antithesis of his father's – a shrewd frugality was replaced by largesse, generosity and merriment. It was not only Henry who made his court so glamorous; he had a beautiful bride too. Catherine of Aragon was the widow of Henry's older brother, Arthur, who had died aged fifteen. What began as a marriage of convenience became a love match, and the royal couple enjoyed a happy relationship for many years.

Henry was greedy for glory in France and led the army there in person, but in 1520 he made peace with Francis I in an ostentatious meeting known as the Field of the Cloth of Gold. In 1518 the Treaty of London was signed in an attempt to bring together the leaders of Europe – England, France, Spain, Burgundy, the Netherlands and the Holy Roman Empire united with the Pope in a non-aggression pact. All of this suggested the dawning of a new age of peace, although it did not last long. Henry left most of the detail of government to Cardinal Wolsey, a butcher's son who was an administrative genius, and who rose to become Lord Chancellor and Archbishop of York. He did, however, greatly improve the royal navy, building some magnificent warships.

Henry's relationship with Catherine was strained by his affairs and by her failure to produce a male heir. From her many pregnancies, only one child survived – a girl, Princess Mary. In 1526 events took a sinister turn for Catherine when Henry fell in love with Anne Boleyn, the sister of one of his former mistresses. Made sophisticated by a stay in France, Anne was shrewd enough to refuse the King the prize he yearned for. Henry became convinced that the lack of a male heir was God's punishment for marrying his brother's widow, and he was so confident that the Pope would grant an annulment that in 1528 he told Anne they would soon be married.

But the Pope was under the control of Catherine's nephew, Emperor Charles V, and despite Wolsey's increasingly desperate attempts, he would not grant Henry a divorce. Wolsey fell from power and was replaced first by Thomas More, who was executed when he refused to support Henry's plans, and later Thomas Cromwell. Henry achieved the divorce he wanted by making the momentous step of taking England out of the Roman Catholic Church and forming the Church of England, with himself at its head. This gave the King licence to dissolve or demolish the rich, unpopular monasteries, which owned about a third of the country, an act which greatly bolstered the royal treasury, although the widespread destruction of monastic libraries caused an immeasurable cultural loss for the nation. Unlike Anne, Cromwell and other supporters of the Crown, however, Henry was in no sense committed to a 'Protestant' Reformation, and lived and died a Catholic, if not a Roman one.

Henry married Anne in 1533, but she too failed to produce the male heir required, giving birth to a daughter, Elizabeth. Henry became convinced that she had used witchcraft to seduce him and that she was an insatiable adulteress. A list of five lovers was compiled, which included her own brother. Subjected to torture, they were forced to admit their guilt and were executed. Anne followed them to the block in 1536. The King then married the gentle Jane Seymour, who produced the much-desired male heir, Edward, but died twelve days later.

Henry next turned to a foreign wife, Anne of Cleves, to help consolidate Protestant alliances, but she was not as pretty as Holbein's portrait of her had suggested and so she was quickly divorced, which was a diplomatic disaster. Cromwell, who had suggested the marriage, was executed for treason. He was not adequately replaced and the gains made earlier in the reign were dissipated with unsuccessful and expensive wars in France and Scotland.

By this time Henry's disposition had become grimmer. He was suspicious to the point of paranoia and his bad temper was exacerbated by a painful leg injury which would not heal and prevented exercise. In his late forties, he married the teenaged Catherine Howard. But she too was accused of adultery and treason and she was executed in 1542. A year later, Henry was married to his sixth and final wife, Catherine Parr, who outlived him.

Henry died in 1547, leaving the throne to his only son, Edward. Although his reign was not as successful as the early years had promised, Henry did leave behind a more united country. Administrative practices in the north and west were aligned with those in the south and helped bring to an end the separatist tendencies in Northumberland, and the over-mighty aristocrats who had caused the Wars of the Roses lost their power base.

Henry had three or four illegitimate children in addition to those by his wives, Mary, Elizabeth and Edward.

EDWARD VI
Reigned 1547–1553

Edward was born in 1537 at Hampton Court. He was a precocious and rather priggish child – serious, scholarly and dedicated to the Protestant religion.

He came to the throne aged ten, on the death of his father. The Council of Regency carefully put together by Henry VIII was overthrown by Edward's uncle, Edward Seymour, who became Duke of Somerset and Lord Protector, supported by Archbishop Cranmer and John Dudley, Earl of Warwick, all of whom were committed to the Reformation.

Cranmer introduced the *Book of Common Prayer*, a Protestant prayer book written in English, in 1548. Changes were made to the sacraments, services had to be held in English and there was widespread destruction of Catholic icons and religious art. But this consolidation of the Protestant Church of England led to Catholic rebellions in the West Country and Norfolk, and in 1549 Somerset was overthrown, and Dudley, who was made Duke of Northumberland, took the lead in government. Somerset was eventually tried for treason and executed.

Dudley tried to involve Edward as much as possible in matters of government, and the young King does appear to have supported the Reformation. How much of this was due to Dudley's influence, however, is not clear because Edward never reached adulthood.

When it became clear in his final year that he would not survive to have children, thoughts turned to the succession. According to Henry VIII's will, next in line to the throne was Edward's eldest sister, Mary, then Elizabeth. Mary, the daughter of Catherine of Aragon, had remained steadfast in her Catholicism, despite pressure from Edward. Edward wanted to save the Protestant religion and Dudley wanted to save himself, so Mary and Elizabeth were excluded and Edward's cousin Lady Jane Grey was made heir to the throne and quickly married to Dudley's son, Guilford.

JANE
Reigned 1553

Jane Grey was born in Bradgate Manor, Leicestershire in 1537, the daughter of the Duke of Suffolk and Lady Frances Brandon. Lady Frances was the daughter of Henry VIII's younger sister, Mary, and so Jane had a claim to the throne. Jane's parents were very stern and she said she was 'so sharply taunted, so cruelly threatened ... with pinches, nips and bobs and other ways ... that I think myself in hell'. As a consequence, Jane was gentle, meek and scholarly, finding solace in her books.

A committed Protestant, Jane was an attractive option for those who did not wish to see the Catholic Princess Mary ascend to the throne, and the Duke of Northumberland and his protégé King Edward VI sought to ensure that she would succeed. She was married to Guilford Dudley, the handsome son of the Duke of Northumberland in 1553, shortly before Edward's death. The wedding and subsequent manoeuvrings were probably much against Jane's will.

Edward died on 6 July 1553 and Jane was proclaimed queen on 10 July. But Edward's death had come sooner than expected and Northumberland was too slow to seize Princess Mary, who fled to

Suffolk. Mary quickly drummed up support for her cause, while Northumberland's supporters deserted him, evidence of popular belief in Mary's legitimacy and rights as heir, regardless of religion. Queen Jane was deposed after only nine days of nominal power and the throne passed to Mary. Jane and Guilford Dudley were imprisoned in the Tower, though Mary's inclination was to be lenient with Jane, as she seemed to have been a largely innocent victim of Northumberland's machinations. However, the outbreak of a rebellion led by Thomas Wyatt forced Mary to act and the unlucky Jane and her husband were beheaded on Tower Green in February 1554. Jane was just seventeen years old.

MARY I
Reigned 1553–1558

Mary was born in 1516 at Greenwich Palace, the only surviving child of Henry VIII and his first wife, Catherine of Aragon. She was made illegitimate when Henry divorced Catherine, but she was restored to the succession towards the end of her father's life when he named her next in line to the throne after her half-brother Edward. Edward tried hard to persuade her to abandon her faith, but to no avail – she remained a dedicated Catholic all her life. When Edward died and the Duke of Northumberland raised the Protestant Lady Jane Grey to the throne, she was in grave danger, but she managed to evade arrest. Most of the English people, commoners and nobles alike, were behind her, and after a few uncertain days she was able to march triumphantly into London to claim her rightful throne. Jane was imprisoned and the Duke of Northumberland was executed.

Mary was thirty-eight when she came to the throne, so it was vital that she marry quickly and produce an heir. She chose her cousin Philip of Spain, the Catholic son of the mighty Holy Roman Emperor Charles V, from a shortlist of eligible princes. Philip was ten years younger and the marriage was not successful. Nor was it popular. In 1554, Sir Thomas Wyatt led an unsuccessful revolt against the marriage in Kent, which forced Mary to act decisively. Lady Jane Grey and her husband, Guilford Dudley, were executed and Mary's Protestant half-sister, Princess Elizabeth, was imprisoned in the Tower for a time.

Mary was committed to the restoration of the Catholic faith, and Parliament set to dismantling the Protestant reforms. Monasteries were reopened and Mass was celebrated again. But the question was whether Mary would revert to Henry's rather watered-down version of Catholicism or go for full-scale Roman Catholicism. She opted for the latter. The laws of heresy were reinstated and Mary's regime became more repressive. First, leading Protestant bishops were burnt at the stake and then over 250 English Protestants, many of them ordinary citizens, earning her the nickname 'Bloody Mary'. The deaths did much to turn the English away from Mary and the Catholic Church. As Catholic exiles returned to England, Protestant exiles fled to Geneva, where a vibrant opposition was set up. Protestant plots abounded.

After a false pregnancy early on in Mary's marriage, an unhappy Philip had departed for Spain. He became King of Spain in 1556, making Mary Queen of Spain as well as England. Mary joined Philip in a disastrous war against France which led to the loss of Calais, the only surviving English territory there. Philip returned to England only once, in 1557. A second false pregnancy ensued, and Mary died in 1558, possibly of stomach cancer. She died a disappointed woman, knowing that the crown would pass to her non-Catholic sister, Elizabeth. Mary's husband did not return to say his goodbyes – he had already turned his attention to marrying Elizabeth.

ELIZABETH I
Reigned 1558–1603

English Protestants rejoiced when Queen Elizabeth came to power, and Catholics returned to exile on the other side of the English Channel. Before she took the throne, Elizabeth had seen unprecedented religious upheaval, with the country swinging from Catholicism to Protestantism and back again. Her genius was that she found a settlement that reconciled the country to the new religion without wholesale violence, creating a myth of the Virgin Queen, nicknamed 'Gloriana' or 'Good Queen Bess', that still has power today.

Elizabeth was born in 1533 in Greenwich Palace, the only surviving child of Anne Boleyn, who had Protestant leanings. Despite the execution of her mother, Elizabeth adored and looked up to her father, Henry VIII. She was very intelligent and well educated, being particularly skilled in foreign languages. With the death of Henry, she entered a dangerous period, as others sought to involve her in dynastic plots and intrigues. As a teenager she was sent to live with her father's sixth wife, the kindly Catherine Parr. When Henry died, Catherine married Thomas Seymour. Seymour would steal kisses from his stepdaughter and was even found to have visited her bedroom. After Catherine's death, Seymour planned to marry Elizabeth as a possible route to power, but his plot was discovered and he was executed. Elizabeth considered him 'a man of much wit and very little judgement'; some have claimed that the 'Seymour affair' left her emotionally scarred for life.

With the accession of Mary to power, the situation became even more dangerous, as Elizabeth was now the heir apparent and a figurehead for those Protestants who hated the Catholic Queen. After Thomas Wyatt's rebellion in 1554, Queen Mary had Elizabeth taken to the Tower and questioned, but she was given the benefit of the doubt and was sent into closely guarded exile in the country.

So, when news came to her of Mary's death in 1558, Elizabeth felt that her survival was 'the Lord's doing'. England was a nation in danger of tearing itself apart over the religious controversy. Elizabeth acted cautiously and established the Church of England, retaining some Catholic traditions, such as a hierarchy of bishops, but reinstating the monarchy as head of the Church and reintroducing the *Book of Common Prayer*. She declared herself against religious persecution, saying that she did not want to make 'windows into men's souls' – she was happy as long as her subjects attended Church of England services. But if they didn't they were heavily fined, and after 1570, when the Pope declared Elizabeth deposed, being an active Catholic became tantamount to being a traitor, and executions – particularly of priests – became more common.

Elizabeth knew how to control Parliament and keep the affection of her people. She was often considered to be very indecisive, wavering particularly over marriage plans, the succession and waging war. But often her prevarication prevented worse problems arising from hasty or wrong decisions. She chose superb and loyal advisors, such as William Cecil (Lord Burghley) and Francis Walsingham, who served her well throughout her reign.

Despite a long procession of eager suitors, Elizabeth never married, although she surrounded herself with handsome courtiers. Her favourite, Robert Dudley, took on the role of consort, and she was enormously fond of him, nicknaming him 'Sweet Robin', though whether there was a sexual element to their relationship will never be known.

With no heir to the throne, Elizabeth's cousin, Mary Queen of Scots, a Catholic descended from Henry VIII's older sister Margaret, was a serious threat. Mary was forced to abdicate from Scotland and fled to England, where she was imprisoned and became the centre of a series of Catholic plots. Finally, it was discovered that a Catholic nobleman called Anthony Babington was planning a coup to kill Elizabeth and put Mary on the throne. In 1587, Mary was beheaded, although Elizabeth agonized over the decision.

Elizabeth hated the waste of war, but in the 1580s war broke out between England and Spain and she approved piratical raids by Francis Drake and others on the Spanish Main. In 1588, the English triumphed over Spain by defeating the Spanish Armada, a formidable invading force. The Queen rallied her troops at Tilbury with her famous and dramatic speech: 'I know I have the body of a weak and feeble woman, but I have the heart and stomach of a king.'

With many of her trusted friends and advisors now dead, Elizabeth found a new favourite in the handsome young Earl of Essex, Robert Devereux. He was shown great favour until he returned without permission from an unsuccessful campaign to put down a rebellion in Ireland in 1599. He was found guilty of dereliction of duty and put under house arrest, whereupon he attempted a farcically unsuccessful coup and was executed in 1601.

After this betrayal, an ageing and tired Elizabeth lost much of her former spark. She had trouble sleeping, fell into a depression and died on 24 March 1603.

THE STUARTS AND THE COMMONWEALTH

❧

The Stuarts were Scottish kings, descended from Robert II, the grandson of Robert the Bruce. Bruce's daughter Marjorie married Walter Stewart (originally Steward) and gave his name to the dynasty. In the sixteenth century, Mary Queen of Scots, herself a Stewart, married Henry Stuart (Lord Darnley), and their son, James I, was the first of the renamed Stuart dynasty. Apart from James I, who was Protestant, the dynasty had a predilection for High Church forms of Christianity. This led to their downfall at the hands of the Puritan Oliver Cromwell, and the monarchy's replacement with England's first republic, known as the Commonwealth. The Stuarts had a slight revival after the Commonwealth ended, withstanding an abdication crisis, but the dynasty petered out when none of Queen Anne's nineteen children from eighteen pregnancies survived childhood.

JAMES I OF ENGLAND; JAMES VI OF SCOTLAND
Reigned 1603–1625

James was not a regal king, being considered rather uncouth, but he was shrewd and well educated, and though he always looked for peaceful solutions, he was not perceived as weak.

He was born in 1566 at Edinburgh Castle, the son of Queen Elizabeth's cousin, Mary Queen of Scots, and Lord Darnley. Less than a year later, his father had been murdered, his Catholic mother forced to abdicate and he had become James VI of Scotland. Although born a Catholic, James was brought up as a Protestant and a series of Protestant regents ruled Scotland during his youth. From an early age he had a preference for handsome men and he was heavily influenced by his favourites at court.

To increase his chance of succeeding the childless Elizabeth as King of England, James established a policy of peace with England. He gave no support to the Spanish or French, and his response to the execution of his mother in England in 1587 was subdued.

Like Elizabeth in England, James sought to keep the peace between Protestants and Catholics in Scotland by treading a middle ground. Given his sexual inclinations, James's marriage to Anne of Denmark in 1589 was surprisingly successful – she became pregnant no fewer than twelve times, although only three of their children survived beyond infancy. James accepted her conversion to Catholicism, despite the fact that it could have had disastrous consequences. Instead, he used her faith to his advantage. Once the English throne was his when Elizabeth died in 1603, the Catholics had hopes of toleration, while Protestants believed that he would bring Calvinism to England. He was well received by the English people, but this initial enthusiasm was soon compromised by the preferment James gave to his Scottish favourites. His middle-ground policy also lost him the support of extreme Catholics and Protestants, and his policy of peace with Spain was unpopular with Parliament and the merchants and Protestants.

James commissioned a new version of the Bible in English to ensure that revolutionary and anti-monarchical references in Puritan translations were removed. His *King James Bible* endured for centuries. Another lasting legacy was the Union 'Jack' flag, introduced in 1606, which James hoped would signify the union of Scotland and England under one king.

In 1605 a group of Catholic hotheads plotted to blow up the King and Parliament when Parliament was opened on 5 November. A warning letter sent to a leading Catholic peer was disclosed to the government and a search of the cellars below the chamber of the House of Lords revealed Guy Fawkes guarding enough barrels of gunpowder to have killed the royal family and both Houses of Parliament. The other plotters were killed or captured after a siege and the survivors were tortured and then hanged, drawn and quartered. The discovery of the Gunpowder Plot encouraged James in his belief in the divine right of kings – namely, that the king had a God-given right to rule and must therefore be obeyed without question.

Towards the end of his life, the ailing King was increasingly under the influence of his new favourite, George Villiers, whom he had made Duke of Buckingham and who was deeply unpopular. He died in 1625, at his palace at Theobalds Park, with Buckingham at his bedside.

CHARLES I
Reigned 1625–1649

Charles had all the attributes of a great king – he was a pious, family man, capable of decisive action as well as compromise. But he combined this with an arrogance and lack of judgement that proved fatal.

He was born in Dunfermline in 1600, the son of James VI of Scotland and Anne of Denmark, and he was just two years old when his father became James I of England. A sickly child, he suffered from rickets, which contributed to his small stature. Not expected to inherit the throne, he was thrust into the limelight when his older brother, Henry, suddenly died. He soon fell under the spell of his father's favourite, the charismatic but unpopular Duke of Buckingham. In 1623 the two of them went on a harebrained and disastrous expedition to Spain to find Charles a bride, which was such an embarrassment that the Spanish ambassador called for Buckingham's execution. Soon after he came to the throne, Charles then antagonized Puritan critics by marrying a French Catholic princess, Henrietta Maria, with whom he went on to have nine children.

At the beginning of his reign, Charles decided to take an active role in the draining Thirty Years War in Europe, undoing his father's policy of peace. The war went badly, directed as it was by the incompetent Buckingham, who also embroiled England in an attack on the French Protestants at La Rochelle. These failures led to an attempt by Parliament to impeach Buckingham, who was assassinated in 1628; Charles then adjourned Parliament in 1629, ruling alone for the next eleven years.

Without the income of parliamentary taxes, Charles used

a variety of unconstitutional methods to raise money, which included the sale of trade monopolies, forced loans, payment for knighthoods, the enlargement of the royal forests and the auctioning of orphan heiresses to the highest bidder. Like his father before him, Charles believed in his divine right to rule and that he must be obeyed without question, which did not sit well with the public. In addition, Charles supported an unpopular High Church vision of the Church of England.

In 1640 Charles was forced to call on Parliament in order to raise money after he was defeated by the Scots in an unnecessary war, caused by his attempt to impose an Anglican prayer book on Scotland. Known as the Short Parliament, it achieved little and was dissolved after a month. A second military defeat forced the calling of a second Parliament, the Long Parliament. This time the Puritan opposition was very well organized and the King was forced to accept laws that turned England into what amounted to a constitutional monarchy. In 1642 Charles attempted a coup and led troops into the House of Commons to arrest the parliamentary leadership. But they had been forewarned and had fled to the City of London, where they were protected by a vociferous mob.

Soon afterwards, Charles raised the royal standard in Nottingham and the Civil War began. The initial success of the Royalists soon ebbed away as the New Model Army, led by Oliver Cromwell, swept all before it, and in 1647 Charles was imprisoned. At this point, Parliament still hoped to reinstate the King, albeit as a pliant constitutional monarch, but Charles continued to negotiate secretly with potential allies. He fled to the Isle of Wight, and in 1648 the short-lived Second Civil War took place. The Royalists were again defeated and Charles was recaptured. This time there were no plans to restore the monarchy. Charles was tried by a special tribunal, the authority of which he refused to recognize, and was beheaded at Whitehall on 30 January 1649. To many he was a martyr but others believe he brought about his own downfall. Either way, he remains the only English king to be tried for treason and executed.

OLIVER CROMWELL AND THE COMMONWEALTH
Ruled 1649–1660

Oliver Cromwell was born in Huntingdon in 1599, a member of the gentry. He became a Member of Parliament in 1628, a short-lived role, as Charles I dissolved this Parliament in 1629 and ruled without it for eleven years. He returned as an MP when Parliament was recalled in 1640.

Cromwell had been converted in his thirties to a radical Puritan philosophy, a form of Protestantism which believed the Reformation had not gone far enough, and opposed the supremacy of the monarch in the Church. He was a member of a tightly knit network of Puritans, many of them cousins, who led the opposition to Charles I leading up to the Civil War. But it was the Civil War that brought Cromwell to prominence. When war was declared in 1642, Cromwell raised a regiment to fight against the King, despite initially having little military experience. He described his recruitment techniques thus: 'I had rather have a plain, russet-coated Captain, that knows what he fights for, and loves what he knows, than that which you call a Gentle-man and is nothing else.'

In 1645 Cromwell was able to force through reforms that led to the formation of the New Model Army, against which the King's hierarchical and poorly funded army could not compete. Through decisive action, Cromwell was able to control his army while defeating opposition from all sides – Royalists, Scots and Irish, and Presbyterians, as well as Levellers, Diggers, Ranters and other radicals who sought power for the ordinary citizen.

At the end of the Civil War, Cromwell led negotiations for a possible restoration of the monarchy, but army leaders became convinced that the negotiations were fruitless. In December 1648 Colonel Pride forcibly purged Parliament of members that supported an agreement with the King, and the remaining MPs of the Rump Parliament, as it became known, agreed that Charles should be tried for treason.

When Charles was executed in 1649, Parliament passed an act that abolished the monarchy and set up the Commonwealth, the only time that England was ever a republic. Cromwell was the leading figure in the Council of State, which ruled the new Commonwealth along with the Rump Parliament. He continued to seek a solution to the constitutional crisis, but the existing electorate would have voted for a new Royalist Parliament, and Cromwell would not countenance extending the electorate as he believed only the propertied classes should be given the vote. Military dictatorship thus seemed the only way forward.

Between 1649 and 1650 Cromwell led a successful but bloody campaign against Irish Catholics who had allied themselves with the defeated Royalists. An equally successful campaign against the Scots, who had given their support to the executed king's son, also called Charles, followed in 1650–51. On his return to England, Cromwell was faced with a troublesome, quarrelling Rump

Parliament, who could not agree what form the new constitution should take. The Rump Parliament was dissolved and replaced in 1653 by the Barebone's Parliament, or Nominated Assembly (as its members were not properly elected); this included Scottish and Irish members but was also dissolved after a short time. In 1653 the Commonwealth was replaced by the Protectorate, in which Cromwell's overwhelming power was recognized in his election for life as Protector. He refused the crown when he was offered it, but he was king in all but name, even being addressed as 'Your Highness'.

Cromwell's successes as a general and as Protector are undoubted. Britain gained a new prestige abroad because of its efficient military forces; opposition in England, Scotland and Ireland was decisively defeated; and religious freedom was successfully extended. But there was no constitutional settlement and the massacre of Catholics in the siege of Drogheda and Wexford in Ireland stain Cromwell's memory. He died in Westminster in 1658 and his son, Richard, briefly took over as Protector. But Richard could not control the army. The Rump Parliament was recalled and Generals Fleetwood and Lambert attempted to continue the Puritan control, but the country had lost faith in the army. Richard resigned in 1659 and Charles I's son was invited to take the throne.

Cromwell was married to Elizabeth Bouchier and had nine children.

CHARLES II
Reigned 1660–1685

Whatever the deficiencies of Charles II as a king, he kept his crown while his father and brother both lost theirs. This speaks much for his likeable personality and his ability to judge public opinion.

He was born in 1630 at St James's Palace in London, the son of Charles I and Henrietta Maria. As a teenager he served with his father's armies in the Civil War for a while, but was sent to his mother in France when the Royalists began to fear defeat. Shortly after his father was executed in 1649, he was crowned King of Scotland, but his attempt to restore the English monarchy with the support of a Scottish army was ended by Cromwell at the Battle of Worcester. Charles spent six dangerous weeks hiding from Cromwell's Roundheads (a name used in reference to the typical Puritan close-cropped hairstyle) before finding a ship to take him back to France.

In 1659 the Protectorate collapsed and negotiations began to restore Charles to the throne, which led to the Declaration of Breda, in which the conditions for Charles's acceptance of the crown were laid out. A pardon was given to all participants in the Civil War except those who had signed Charles I's death warrant, and a new Royalist Parliament was elected. On 29 May 1660, a triumphant Charles arrived in London, to be greeted by enthusiastic crowds who were thrilled to see the end of the grim Puritan regime. According to contemporary observer John Evelyn: 'This day came in his Majestie Charles the 2d to London after a sad and long exile ... the ways strawed with flowers, the bells ringing, the streets hung with tapistry, fountains running with wine ... All this without one drop of blood ... it was the Lord's doing ...' Cromwell's body was dug up and hanged at Tyburn and the regicides hanged, drawn and quartered.

The scenes of celebration that greeted Charles's arrival in London set the tone for the rest of his reign. Charles had an easy charm, a lazy disposition and a roving eye, and he loved frivolity, extravagance and pretty women. He had many mistresses – including the high-spirited actress Nell Gwyn who called herself the 'Protestant Whore' to differentiate herself from the French Catholic Louise de Kéroualle, whom she nicknamed 'Squintabella'. He fathered sixteen illegitimate children, but his wife, Catherine of Braganza, failed to provide him with an heir. He was interested in science and patronized the Royal Society which, with Robert Hooke, Isaac Newton and Christopher Wren as its members, set in place the foundations for Britain's leading role in the development of the sciences.

But Charles's reign had many difficulties. He had to deal with the devastation wreaked by the plague in 1665 and the Great Fire of London in 1666. There were serious divisions between Catholics, Anglicans and Puritans that threatened to destabilize the country. Anti-Catholic feelings ran high and Charles's decision to ally with Louis XIV against the Dutch was unpopular. With no heir and a Catholic brother, James, set to inherit, Charles had to show his mettle against the Protestants in Parliament, the Whigs, who tried to exclude James from the throne. That Charles succeeded in preserving James's inheritance without starting another civil war is one of his main achievements. Charles died in Whitehall Palace in 1685 from a stroke.

JAMES II
Reigned 1685–1688

Unlike his brother, Charles II, James learned all the wrong lessons from the execution of his father. He was aloof, arrogant and believed compromise was a fatal sign of weakness. He therefore lost his kingdom, to his own daughter, Mary, and son-in-law, William.

James was born in 1633 at St James's Palace in London. He was captured by the Roundheads in 1646, but managed to escape in 1648, disguised as a girl. He spent the next few years in exile, but he returned to England when his brother was restored to the throne in 1660. He had considerable experience of command, having served in the English, French and Spanish armies, and was made Lord High Admiral. Like his brother, he had widespread affairs and in 1660 was forced to marry Anne Hyde, daughter of the Earl of Clarendon, as she was pregnant. She went on to bear him eight children, but only two daughters, Mary and Anne, survived. James converted to Catholicism in the 1660s, which caused his brother tremendous difficulties. In 1673, James was forced to resign from office and went into exile briefly. When Anne died, he married the devoutly Catholic Mary of Modena, which further antagonized his Protestant opponents.

When Charles died in 1685, the country initially rallied to James, and Parliament supported him in the face of a dangerous Protestant rebellion led by Charles's bastard son, the Duke of Monmouth. The revolt was brutally suppressed and James had his nephew Monmouth beheaded.

James sought to remove anti-Catholic laws by a policy of religious toleration. He expanded the army and forced the appointment of

Catholics to prominent positions. The problem was that he pushed his reforms through too quickly. This alarmed the Protestants, who feared a king with a standing army bent on the restoration of Catholicism, which was linked in British minds with totalitarian rule. The situation deteriorated alarmingly when Mary of Modena, succeeding with her eleventh pregnancy, bore him a son, James. Protestants claimed the pregnancy was false and that another baby had been smuggled into the birthing room in a warming pan. Those who had been happy to accept a Catholic king in his late middle age felt that a Catholic dynasty threatened the end of the Church of England. English bishops refused to support James's policy of tolerance and were imprisoned in the Tower, and anti-Catholic rioting took place in London and elsewhere.

To force a solution, leading Protestant lords invited James's Protestant daughter, Mary, to take the throne. In November 1688 her husband and first cousin, William of Orange, landed in Torbay with an invasion force and marched slowly towards London. As they marched, James's support gradually melted away. Eventually, he lost confidence and fled, although he was soon captured and returned to London. William encouraged him to go into exile and he was allowed to leave for France, effectively abdicating the throne. In 1690, James made an attempt to reclaim the crown with the support of the Catholic Irish, but his forces were crushed by William at the Battle of the Boyne and he returned to exile in France, where he died in 1701.

MARY II
Reigned 1689–1694

AND WILLIAM III
Reigned 1689– 1702

William and Mary are the only couple in British history who reigned as joint monarchs. When Mary was asked to take the throne on the abdication of her father, James II, in 1688, she insisted that her husband and cousin William should rule with her. As William was James II's nephew and was third in line to the throne after Mary and her sister Anne, this was considered acceptable.

As Stadtholder of Holland, William was one of the leading Protestants in Europe. His marriage to Mary in 1677 sealed an alliance between two Protestant powers which had only recently been at war. The accession of Mary's Catholic father, James II, to the throne of England in 1685 created some difficulties, but William sent troops to help James crush the Duke of Monmouth's Protestant rebellion. However, by 1688 further concessions to Catholicism had alarmed the English and leading Protestant aristocrats invited William and Mary to take the throne.

William's decision to invade in November of that year with some 20,000 troops was a brave one. The chances of a disastrous storm were high at that time of year and the welcome he would receive in England was entirely uncertain. But there was no storm and the invasion was unopposed – in fact the Glorious Revolution was a resounding success. In London, Mary and William accepted the Bill of Rights, which provided that the monarchy should be Protestant, that Parliament should be called regularly, that there should be no standing army without parliamentary permission, and that no monarch should dispense or suspend English laws. This in effect established England as a constitutional monarchy, although the monarch remained the leading power in the land, still with the power to veto new laws suggested by Parliament.

William's chief foreign policy was the war against France. He met opposition from Tory MPs, who resented the high taxation needed to pursue a war that some felt benefited Holland more than England. William spent long periods of his reign in Ireland, leaving Mary to rule in his absence.

The formation of the Bank of England in 1694 and the creation of the National Debt solved the financial crisis that had handicapped English monarchs from the fifteenth century to the end of the seventeenth century. It has been suggested that the National Debt was a necessary precondition of the formation of the British Empire, which required the defeat of France in Canada, the West Indies and India.

Mary died of smallpox in 1694, leaving no surviving children. After her death, her sister Anne allowed William to continue to reign, and he did so until his death in 1702.

ANNE
Reigned 1702–1714

Anne was born in 1665 at St James's Palace to James II and his first wife, Anne Hyde. She was brought up as a Protestant, and in 1683 she married Prince George of Denmark, another northern European Protestant power. Her mother died when she was very young and her father married the Catholic Mary of Modena, whom Anne disliked. She played an important part in the fall of her father by giving credence to rumours that her stepmother had secretly switched her stillborn baby with someone else's live one in order to secure a Catholic dynasty. She fed information to her older sister Mary and her husband, William of Orange, about James II's deteriorating position, and she knew that William was preparing to invade in 1688, but did not warn her father. When the invasion proved successful, she gave her permission for William to become joint monarch with her sister, and when Mary died she set aside her claim to the throne until William died.

After William's death in 1702 she finally became queen, with Prince George as her consort. George remained very much in the background. William III once said of him, 'I've tried him drunk and I've tried him sober but there's nothing in him,' but by all accounts Anne and George had a happy, loving marriage. Plain and increasingly plump, Anne did not cut a regal figure, but she was good-natured and generous, and she was much loved by her subjects. She conceived at least nineteen children, but sadly only one, William, survived for any length of time, and he too died at the age of eleven.

Anne was involved in one of the most famous royal friendships. Sarah Jennings, later the wife of the Duke of Marlborough, became Anne's favourite and they used to address each other as Mrs Morley and Mrs Freeman in correspondance, to avoid the tedious formality normally required between sovereign and subject.

Perhaps the most important legacy of Anne's rule was England's political union with Scotland, which was masterminded by her Whig government. The Acts of Union were passed by both Scottish and English Parliaments in 1707, which merged both kingdoms and their Parliaments. Robert Burns wrote about the widespread bribery necessary to persuade the Scots to the Union: 'We were bought and sold for English gold.' England and Scotland had had the same monarchs since the accession of James I in 1603, but now the two countries were united as the Kingdom of Great Britain.

Anne's reign was also dominated by the War of Spanish Succession, with England supporting Archduke Charles in his efforts to claim the Spanish throne. She placed the brilliant Duke of Marlborough in charge of English forces, and he had success after success. The Battle of Blenheim in 1704 is considered to be one of the turning points in European history, one that prevented France from dominating Europe. As the war became more unpopular at home, Anne fell out with her Whig supporters and turned to the Tories instead, forcing Marlborough out of power. However, the war ended in 1713, with the Treaty of Utrecht, with Britain gaining some considerable territory in North America and the right to ship slaves to the Spanish colonies. Anne died a year later in 1714 due to complications from gout.

THE HOUSE OF HANOVER

❧

George the First was always reckon'd
Vile – but viler George the Second;
And what mortal ever heard
Any good of George the Third?
When from earth the Fourth descended,
God be praised, the Georges ended.

W. S. Landor

This poem may be a little cruel but the Georges were not popular. Germans from Hanover, they only got the job because they were Protestant. William IV was perhaps the most pleasant of them, but it was Queen Victoria who undoubtedly saved the dynasty's reputation and restored respect for the royals. However, as a woman she could not rule Hanover itself, which became once more independent of England. Victoria married Albert of Saxe-Coburg-Gotha, another small independent state in Germany, thus renaming the dynasty. This name stayed in use until the First World War, through the reign of Edward VII and part of the reign of George V.

GEORGE I
Reigned 1714–1727

George was born in Hanover in 1660 to the Duke of Brunswick and Sophia Stuart. He was fifty-eighth in line to the throne when Queen Anne died, but the first fifty-seven were Catholic, so the throne was passed to him as the senior member of the Protestant branch of the family, which was descended from James I's daughter, Elizabeth.

George would rather have stayed in Hanover, and the British were less than delighted with a fifty-four-year-old king who could speak virtually no English. He had proved his leadership qualities in battle and government back in Hanover, but he was perceived as dull, lacking in appropriate manners and used to unlimited power. He kept his beautiful but unfaithful wife, Sophia Dorothea, with whom he had two children, incarcerated until her death, and he was accused of murdering her lover. He brought his German mistress, Melusine von der Schulenburg (nicknamed 'Maypole' because she was very tall and thin), to England and fathered three royal bastards by her. His half-sister, Baroness Sophia von Kielmansegg, was also alleged to be his lover. She was nicknamed 'the Elephant' as she was short and fat.

Despite the criticisms against him, however, George evidently had a cool head, because he steered the country through a series of difficult crises. He stood firm during the Jacobite uprising of 1715, when the Scots rose in support of the Catholic James Stuart, the Old Pretender, son of James II. Riots broke out in major cities and an invasion force marched as far south as Preston in Lancashire, failed to raise sufficient recruits and was easily defeated in the last battle ever to take place on English soil.

The rebellion had been supported by many Tories, leaving the King dependent upon the Whigs. His lack of familiarity with the British system, poor grasp of English and frequent trips to Hanover increased the independence of his ministers, although George still insisted on controlling foreign affairs and exercised his powers of patronage to influence Parliament. He was further weakened by the creation of an opposition of dissident Whigs that formed around the King's son, Prince George, who hated his father for locking up his mother.

In the face of widespread disgust at corruption and amid continuing Jacobite plots, a Whig politician, Robert Walpole, presided over a reconciliation between the King and his son. After skilfully handling the South Sea Bubble crisis of 1720 – when the South Sea Company collapsed, ruining many investors – Walpole helped re-establish confidence in the economy, government and monarchy. His position became almost unassailable, and a fundamental shift in the balance of power in government took place. The King had been actively in charge of government; now Walpole was the 'prime minister' (originally a title of abuse), working with a cabinet and taking advice but not orders from the monarch. Nonetheless, to stay in power he needed to retain the King's confidence, as well as Parliament's.

In 1727, the King returned to Hanover to arrange his wife's burial – seven months after her death – but he died en route after a stroke. Nobody bothered to bring his body back for a state funeral.

GEORGE II
Reigned 1727–1760

George was born in 1683 in Hanover, the son of George I and Sophia Dorothea. He was brought up as a German prince. He was naturalized as a British citizen in 1705 and, unlike his father, he spoke English, albeit with a strong German accent. He was not particularly bright or hard-working but he left most of the decision-making to his government, which laid the foundations for the world's greatest empire.

He married Caroline of Ansbach in 1705, a wise choice as she was bright, beautiful, put up with his mistresses without complaint and was popular with her English subjects. She had ten pregnancies but only seven surviving children. It was said that she was the real power behind the throne:

You may strut, dapper George, but 'twill all be in vain,

We all know 'tis Queen Caroline, not you, that reign.

However, she could not help George get on with his father. They had a terrible relationship and eventually, after a public row at the christening of a short-lived son, George set up a rival court at Leicester House and gathered together opposition to his father's government.

When George became king on the death of his father in 1727, Robert Walpole continued as prime minister of a Whig government, with the support of the influential Caroline. Walpole followed a policy of peace and secured majorities in Parliament by judicious use of patronage and bribery. But in 1740 Britain, against Walpole's better instincts, became embroiled in the War of Austrian Succession, allying with Austria against France, Prussia and Spain, largely in order to reduce France's power. Eventually the war became unpopular – it was felt that Britain's involvement was because of the King's Hanoverian connection, as Hanover was threatened by a French invasion – and Walpole was forced out in 1742. George was the last king to personally lead his army to war, at the Battle of Dettingen in 1743.

In 1745 the French retaliated by supporting the Young Pretender's bid for the throne. Charles Edward Stuart, aka Bonnie Prince Charlie, James II's grandson, landed in Scotland to restore the Stuart's position that had been lost following James II's abdication. With the support of the Highland forces, he defeated the British troops at the Battle of Prestonpans. They pressed on into England, but turned back at Derby. Back in Scotland, at Culloden, the Duke of Cumberland (George's younger son) led a largely professional army, which destroyed the ill-disciplined and ill-equipped Scottish army. Those who fled were hunted down and executed or imprisoned, though Charlie escaped.

George's relationship with his eldest son, Frederick, the Prince of Wales, was uncannily similar to the one he had with his own father – they hated each other. Frederick set up his own rival court at Leicester House, where he opposed everything his father did. George was said to have been glad when Frederick died from a burst lung abscess after being hit by a cricket or tennis ball.

George took even more of a back seat during his later years, allowing the Whig government, dominated by William Pitt the Elder, to run the country and develop Britain into the world's leading colonial power, with the defeat of France in Canada, the West Indies and India. He died in 1760 at Kensington Palace of a stroke, while on the lavatory.

GEORGE III
Reigned 1760–1820

George III was Britain's longest-reigning male monarch and the first of the Georges to be born and raised in England. Nicknamed 'Farmer George', he was generally a good, hard-working man who was devoted to his German wife Charlotte and his fifteen children, and genuinely enjoyed spending time with his subjects. But he was responsible for the worst foreign relations disaster in British history and spent a good portion of his reign mentally incapable of governing the country.

George was the son of Frederick, Prince of Wales, and he succeeded his grandfather George II. Unlike his German predecessors, his understanding of the English system led him to want to govern the country in the traditional manner of English kings. Unfortunately, this was in conflict with recent trends and Whig ideas, and a period of weak government and some calamitous decisions ensued, such as those which resulted in the loss of Britain's thirteen colonies in North America. The King felt that the colonists should help pay for the costs of the Seven Years War, which had forced the French out of North America. A stamp duty tax and then a tax on tea led from small token resistance to a full-scale and well-organized secession movement.

In late 1783 matters were improved when William Pitt the Younger became prime minister at the age of twenty-four. There followed nearly fifty years of general political continuity, with Pitt and Lord Liverpool acting as prime minister for a total of thirty-four years between them. This stability reinforced the idea that the government of the country was the responsibility of the prime minister and his cabinet, who reported to Parliament.

In foreign policy, George's reign was dominated by the issue of American independence and the Napoleonic Wars, which saw Britain fighting for survival. The famous victories against the French at Trafalgar and Waterloo emphasized a changing role for Britain as the world's leading power.

On the domestic front, the excesses of the French Revolution and fears of a British follow-up led to a curtailment of Britain's famous liberties – the suspension of *habeas corpus* (protection against unlawful detainment) and the banning of trade unions. An Irish independence movement was savagely put down and Ireland was incorporated into the renamed United Kingdom. King George personally prevented William Pitt from allowing Catholics the vote, so the new Irish contingent in Parliament was exclusively Protestant, and Catholics were excluded, with disastrous long-term consequences. On the bright side, however, the beginnings of the agricultural and industrial revolutions led to Britain dominating the production of goods in a way that had never been seen before.

George suffered from his first bout of madness in 1788, when he was reportedly seen talking to a tree, thinking that it was the King of Prussia. He recovered, but his mental faculties were never the same again, and in 1811 he slipped into terminal madness, whereupon his son George became regent. It has been suggested he was suffering from porphyria, a mental illness sometimes triggered by arsenic (which was present in a popular remedy that George took). He lingered on until 1820, when he died of pneumonia.

GEORGE IV
Reigned 1820–1830

George IV was a man of great taste and was one of the greatest royal connoisseurs of art and culture. He was often warm and generous, but he was also selfish, lazy, gluttonous, licentious and extravagant. He was very unpopular and became a figure of fun, often being referred to as the 'Prince of Whales' due to his size. George III was appalled by his son's profligate lifestyle and his early support for the liberal policies of Charles James Fox and the Whigs.

George had many sexual liaisons from an early age. When he was in his early twenties he fell in love with the widowed Maria Fitzherbert, and in 1785 he married her in secret, knowing that the marriage was illegal, as she was Catholic and he was therefore contravening the Royal Marriages Act.

By 1795 George had run up shockingly huge debts and was forced by his father to marry his cousin, Caroline of Brunswick. They disliked each other from the moment they met. She was astonished that he was so fat, in contrast to his handsome portrait. In turn, her coarseness and poor hygiene appalled him (her underwear was apparently 'never well washed or changed often enough'). On their wedding night George was so drunk that he had to leave the bedchamber. The next morning, for 'the only time they were together as husband and wife', they conceived Princess Charlotte. The couple soon separated. George tried to arrange a divorce on the grounds of her adultery, but this disgusted the public, who accused George of hypocrisy on account of his many liaisons, so the proceedings were abandoned.

In 1811 George became Prince Regent when his father's mental illness grew worse. He initiated some major building projects, working in particular with the architect John Nash. In 1815 they created the gorgeous Royal Pavilion at George's seaside property in Brighton and they developed Regent Street and Regent's Park, which were lined with magnificent villas. Once George was king, Buckingham Palace and Windsor Castle were modernized and he persuaded the government to set up the National Gallery.

When George III died in 1820, George IV planned a magnificent coronation which was almost ruined by the arrival of Caroline to claim her role as queen. She was literally shut out of the celebrations, as the doors of Westminster Abbey were locked against her on the undeniable grounds that she had no ticket. Soon after she fell ill. When George was told, on the death of Napoleon, 'I have, Sire, to congratulate you: your greatest enemy is dead,' George replied, 'Is she, by God!' Caroline did in fact die shortly afterwards, claiming to have been poisoned.

When in power, George changed his political allegiance to the Tories, and went from supporting Catholic emancipation to blocking it. Only after the resignation of the entire cabinet in 1829 was the Prime Minister, the Duke of Wellington, able to force the King to sign the Catholic Relief Act, which allowed Catholics to sit in Parliament.

During George's reign public demands for the vote increased and were met with repression, including the infamous Peterloo Massacre in which the Cavalry charged a defenceless crowd, resulting in 700 casualties.

George's drunkenness and gluttony increased during his final years. When drunk he was wont to claim participation in a famous charge at the Battle of Waterloo. He would shout to Wellington, 'Was that not so?' To which Wellington would reply, 'I have often heard Your Majesty say so.' He died in 1830 at Windsor Castle, from a burst blood vessel in his stomach.

WILLIAM IV
Reigned 1830–1837

William IV, according to his obituary in *The Times*, 'was not a man of talent ... but he had a warm heart, and it was an English heart'. Born in 1765 at Buckingham Palace, he was the third son of George III. As he was not expected to be king, he entered the navy at the age of thirteen. He served with some distinction in America and the West Indies, earning Horatio Nelson's approbation. In 1789 he was made Rear Admiral, but spoke up against the war with France and thereafter was not involved in the Napoleonic Wars. Eventually his brother George, who was Prince Regent at the time, made him Lord High Admiral, and he achieved some reforms in this post, including the banning of the use of the brutal cat o' nine tails for routine punishments.

'Sailor Billy' had his share of love affairs: in Hanover he was reportedly seen 'with a lady of the town against a wall'. In the early 1790s William began a long relationship with an Irish actress, Dorothea Jordan, with whom he had ten illegitimate children. But in 1811, under pressure from his mother, the couple split. In 1817 William's niece, Princess Charlotte, died in childbirth. As Charlotte had been next in line to the throne and George IV and his estranged wife had no other heirs, George's brothers began to look for suitable wives. William married Adelaide of Saxe-Meiningen in 1818, but none of their children survived infancy. It was, however, a happy marriage. When William found out he had become king on the death of his brother in 1830, he went straight back to bed so that he could experience the thrill of sleeping with a queen.

As king, he was soon faced with a constitutional crisis when a Whig government committed to extending the vote came to power.

William did not support the proposed Reform Bill, but was forced to ensure that the House of Lords accepted it. This was the first great extension of the vote (though in fact it only extended the electorate from fourteen per cent to eighteen per cent of the population), and it ended the scandal of the so-called rotten boroughs, places where few, if any, people lived but which were represented by an MP, while areas with huge populations had no MP.

William's reign also saw the beginnings of major social reform in Britain, with the passing of the Poor Law Amendment Act, which reformed the poverty relief system, and the abolition of slavery and child labour. William spoke against the abolition of slavery, however, saying that crofters in the Highlands were worse off than slaves in the Caribbean and calling notable abolitionist William Wilberforce a 'fanatic and hypocrite'. He was the last king to choose a prime minister against the will of Parliament, replacing Lord Melbourne with Sir Robert Peel.

William IV died of pneumonia in 1837 at Windsor Castle.

VICTORIA
Reigned 1837–1901

Queen Victoria is the second-longest-reigning British monarch, at sixty-three years and seven months. Her hard work and exemplary family life restored the reputation of the monarchy, although there was major criticism of the Queen for the extended period of mourning she went into after her beloved husband Albert's death. Contrary to her dour reputation, Victoria was not prudish and solemn, but vivacious and high-spirited, at least in the early years of her reign.

Victoria was born in 1819 at Kensington Palace, London. Her father, the Duke of Kent, the fourth son of George III, died when she was eight months old and she was brought up by her mother and the head of her household, Sir John Conroy. Conroy was very controlling and seemed intent on exploiting his role as companion to the Duchess of Kent. Victoria detested him and his influence on her mother.

William IV died in 1837 and an eighteen-year-old Victoria took the throne. She immediately removed herself from the influence of Conroy and her mother. Instead, she enthusiastically adopted the Prime Minister, Lord Melbourne, as her political tutor, earning herself the nickname 'Mrs Melbourne' because of all the time they spent together. When Robert Peel and the Tories came to power in 1839, he insisted she replace her Whig ladies of the chamber with Tories. Victoria refused, causing a constitutional crisis, and Melbourne was recalled.

In 1840 a marriage to her first cousin, Albert of Saxe-Coburg-Gotha, was arranged. For Victoria, it was love at first sight: Albert, she said, had 'the most pleasing and delightful exterior and appearance'. Together they worked very hard to fulfil the role of a constitutional monarchy, but Albert was never popular in England, despite the huge success of his pet project, the Great Exhibition of 1851, which six million visitors from all over the world visited to marvel at the best of British technology and design. Together, Albert and Victoria had nine children, all but one of whom married into the princely dynasties and ruling families of Europe, making her the 'grandmother' of the continent.

Victoria and Albert were effective figureheads during the traumas of the Indian Mutiny and the Crimean War, but in 1861, at the age of forty-two, Albert died of typhoid fever. Victoria blamed her eldest son, Albert Edward (Bertie), for his death, believing it was brought on by stress caused by his liaison with an actress. She was heartbroken and went into a long period of isolation, refusing to undertake her public duties, for which she was heavily criticized.

After a decade she was coaxed back into a more active public role. Victoria had very decided opinions, in particular with regard to foreign policy (as she was related to most of the royal families in Europe, she could claim some special expertise). She also had strong opinions about her prime ministers, loving Melbourne and Disraeli and loathing Gladstone and Palmerston. The monarch's role, however, was bound to diminish, as Prime Ministers Gladstone and Disraeli increased the electorate, so that by the late 1880s there was virtually universal male suffrage.

In 1876, Disraeli – who once said of flattering royalty that 'you should lay it on with a trowel' – made Victoria Empress of India. She fully supported the imperial expansion policy of Lord Salisbury, her last prime minister, which saw Britain participate in the 'Scramble for Africa'.

In later life she had two controversial friendships with servants. The most important was with John Brown, a ghillie at her Balmoral estate. Her affection for him was such that when she died in 1901 she was buried with a lock of his hair and Brown's mother's wedding ring in one hand and Albert's dressing gown in the other. After Brown's death in 1883, she had a close relationship with an Indian servant, Abdul Karim, who taught her Hindi.

The Victorian period saw a massive expansion of the British Empire, the first sustained increase in life expectancy, a substantial increase in urban populations and scientific and technological advances that led to innovations such as train travel, telegraphs, telephones, submarines and the machine gun.

EDWARD VII
Reigned 1901–1910

Edward had to wait sixty years to become king, and although he had been Prince of Wales since his infancy, his mother denied him the chance to play a significant role in state affairs. But he is claimed as the first king of England to embrace the modern constitutional role of strict non-interference in politics, and he was a very popular monarch.

Prince Albert Edward was born in 1841 at Buckingham Palace, the eldest son of Victoria and Albert. He was given a good education, but soon became a disappointment to his parents, who set impossible standards. Victoria believed he was responsible for the death of her beloved Albert after he became involved with an actress. She wrote: 'I never can ... look at him without a shudder.' Edward loved to live the aristocratic lifestyle of shows, fine dining, drinking, horse racing, shooting and sailing. He was associated with numerous glamorous women, such as the beautiful actresses Lily Langtry and Sarah Bernhardt. His wife, Alexandra of Denmark, seems to have accepted his affairs and even invited his most faithful mistress, Alice Keppel (great-grandmother of Camilla Parker-Bowles), to see Edward one last time when he was on his deathbed.

But at the same time Edward was, as Disraeli said, 'informed, intelligent and of a sweet manner'. His avuncular attitude and his skill in foreign relations are remembered in his sobriquet 'Uncle of Europe' and 'the Peacemaker'. His successful tour of India in 1876 led to his mother being offered the title of Empress of India.

When Queen Victoria died in 1901, her son refused to take the name Albert as king, as he felt that only his father deserved to use that illustrious name – and he also wished to take the name of an English king. But as King Edward he played his role with distinction. He is said to have been the first heir to come to the throne without debt, and the public were enthusiastic for a new, livelier royal regime. He was particularly involved with foreign affairs, and his numerous tours abroad were often instrumental in improving diplomatic relations. For example, he helped seal the 1904 Entente Cordiale and therefore the alliance between the UK, France and Russia. He also helped to reform the British Armed Forces, something that was shown to be necessary by the Boer Wars and the increasing threat from Germany. Knowing his nephew, the Kaiser Wilhelm, Edward feared he would bring Europe to war.

All in all, Edward managed the transition into the twentieth century well. He died in 1910 at Buckingham Palace, after suffering several heart attacks. He and Alexandra left five surviving children.

THE HOUSE OF WINDSOR

༃

In 1917 the House of Saxe-Coburg-Gotha was renamed the House of Windsor by George V, because of the rising anti-German sentiment as the horrors of the First World War continued. The King's cousins, the Battenbergs, also changed their name to Mountbatten. Although this may seem like an early piece of political correctness, the new name symbolized a new, more democratic approach by the royal family. By the reign of George V, English monarchs had embraced their constitutional role, their status as a figurehead and their voluntary abstinence from interference in the politics of the nation. They may have been mostly conservative in their outlook and probably in their personal politics, but they hid this from public view, finding a way of surviving without being seen as too much of an anachronism. Where the future of the monarchy lies in an age of divorce, celebrity stardom and the Internet remains to be seen.

GEORGE V
Reigned 1910–1936

Sir Harold Nicholson once said of George V: 'For seventeen years he did nothing at all but kill animals and stick in stamps.' George's ambition was to have the best stamp album in Britain and, although an animal-lover, he once shot 1,000 pheasants in six hours. He was, however, a popular king – he was calm, straightforward and a moderating influence in times of national crisis.

George V was born in 1865 at Marlborough House in London. As he was only the second son of Edward VII, he was allowed to join the navy and lead a relatively normal life. After the unexpected death of his older brother Albert, he married Albert's fiancée, Mary of Teck. The marriage was quite happy, producing six children, and the two of them were the epitome of royal dignity. Sir Henry Channon said of Mary: 'Her appearance was formidable; her manner, well, it was like talking to St Paul's Cathedral.' Mary was of considerable help to her husband, advising him on his speeches and matters of state.

Politically, George was less resistant to change than his father. In 1906 he campaigned for the greater involvement of Indians in government. At the beginning of his reign, he upheld the supremacy of the House of Commons by threatening to create peers to force Lloyd George's People's Budget through the House of Lords. He expressed his horror at the violence that took place as the Irish Free State came into existence. In 1924 he accepted the first Labour government, under Ramsay MacDonald, saying, 'My grandfather would have hated it, my father could hardly have tolerated it, but I march with the times.' During the General Strike of 1926, he urged the government to be moderate in their dealings with the trade unions, saying, 'Try living on their wages' to those who claimed the strikers were revolutionaries. During his reign, the franchise was given to all men and women over the age of twenty-one, and the Dominions were given effective independence from Britain.

During the First World War, George helped as much as he could by visiting the front, hospitals and organizations important to the war effort. He and Mary also tried to avoid an ostentatious lifestyle. In 1917, to appease anti-German feeling, they changed the name of their dynasty from Saxe-Coburg-Gotha to Windsor (Kaiser Wilhelm once joked that he was going to see Shakespeare's *Merry Wives of Saxe-Coburg-Gotha*). At the end of the war, as the old regimes were destroyed, he felt he had to involve himself in rescuing dethroned relatives, but he was obliged to leave the Romanovs of Russia to their fate for fear of political consequences.

As a father, he was strict – 'My father was frightened of his mother, I was frightened of my father and I am damned well going to see to it that my children are frightened of me.' He was not impressed by his eldest son, Edward, and prayed that the crown would go to his younger son, Bertie, the future George VI, and his granddaughter, Elizabeth.

George V died in 1936 at Sandringham of bronchitis. His physician apparently hastened the end to prevent more strain on the family and so the announcement could appear in the morning edition of *The Times*.

EDWARD VIII
Reigned 1936

Edward VIII was born in 1894 at White Lodge, Richmond. He was badly affected by the isolated upbringing typical in the British royal family. He once described his mother as having ice in her veins, although there are reports of the Queen playing tenderly with her children. His father, however, certainly thought little of Edward's potential as a king.

Edward was handsome and sporty. He attended the Royal Naval College and later served in the Grenadier Guards, but he was not allowed to serve at the front during the First World War, much to his regret. After the war, he went on a series of very successful tours of the empire – Canada, the Caribbean, Australia, New Zealand and India – as well as the US, where he was extremely popular. Always fashionably dressed and very photogenic, he became a media star. He conducted a number of affairs, particularly with married women, which added to the playboy reputation that further estranged him from his father.

In 1931 he met and fell in love with Wallis Simpson, a married American woman who already had one divorce under her belt, and they became lovers. She was beautifully dressed, witty and confident. Images of them together began to appear in the American newspapers, although the British media deferentially remained silent on the subject.

When George V died in 1936 and Edward became king, he told the Prime Minister, Stanley Baldwin, that he intended to marry Wallis, who had started divorce proceedings against her second husband. Baldwin told him that the head of the Church of England could not marry a divorcée, a hard line that might have been influenced by the fact that Wallis was suspected of leaking information to the Nazis and having other lovers, including the Nazi ambassador to London, Joaquim von Ribbentrop.

Edward could not accept this, although Wallis offered to give him up. Further negotiations took place. Baldwin presented the case to the prime ministers of the dominions, who made it clear that they would not accept the marriage. Edward, told that he could not marry and stay king, decided to abdicate. His heartfelt announcement was broadcast to the nation, though he was not allowed to broadcast an earlier appeal to his people.

Edward and Wallis went to France, where they were married in June 1937. They paid a visit to Hitler in Germany, and when France fell the British government became concerned about contact with Nazi agents and Edward was sent to the Bahamas as Governor in order to get him out of the way. After the war, Wallis and Edward lived a fashionable but ultimately empty life and relations with the royal family were never fully mended. Edward died in 1972 of cancer at his house in Paris and was buried at Frogmore, Windsor. Wallis was interred next to him when she died in 1986. The couple had no children.

GEORGE VI
Reigned 1936–1952

George VI epitomized the public service ethos of the House of Windsor. Like his father but unlike his brother, he sacrificed much for the throne. Although a shy man, he helped lead the nation successfully through the trauma of the Second World War, and was much-loved by his people.

George VI, known to his family as Bertie, was born in 1895 at Sandringham, the second son of George V and Mary of Teck. He was shy on account of his bad stammer, suffered from knock knees and stomach ulcers, and was 'easily frightened and prone to tears'. This may have been due to the neglect he suffered at the hands of his nurse, who mostly ignored him. As the King's second son, he was allowed to see action during the First World War, in the Battle of Jutland, as a naval officer.

Despite his natural timorousness, he could be determined at times. He pursued Elizabeth Bowes-Lyon for two years before she consented to marry him, and he worked hard on his stammer and his shyness so that he could perform his necessary royal duties. At heart he was a family man who would have preferred a normal life with his wife and daughters. The marriage was unusual in that it was not arranged, and Elizabeth was the perfect complement to him. She was gracious, witty, hard-working and put people at ease.

George was horrified when his brother, Edward VIII, abdicated in 1936. He felt totally unprepared for the role of king, but his sense of duty was strong and he was determined to do a good job. Before the war, he went on important diplomatic tours of France, the USA and Canada. Although the King was originally in favour of trying to appease Nazi Germany, he staunchly supported Churchill as Prime Minister and the two had a good working relationship.

George and Elizabeth played a crucial role in keeping morale high during the war. Despite the dangers, George decided to stay in London, and the Queen and their two daughters refused to leave without him. They were often seen out and about in war-torn London, inspecting the damage caused by bombing and sympathizing and comforting those who had lost homes and loved ones. Elizabeth was glad when Buckingham Palace was bombed in September 1940, saying, 'I feel we can look the East End in the face.' On one occasion, a member of the crowd shouted at George, 'Thank God for a good king,' to which he replied, 'Thank God for a good people.'

After the war, the King had a good relationship with Clement Attlee, as the Labour Party introduced the welfare state, and the royal family adapted well to the transition from Empire to Commonwealth.

George died of cancer in 1952 at Sandringham, leaving his wife and two daughters, Elizabeth and Margaret.

ELIZABETH II
Reigned 1952–present

As of September 2015, Queen Elizabeth II is the United Kingdom's longest-reigning monarch, currently at over sixty-three years on the throne. She has overtaken Elizabeth I (forty-four years), Henry III (fifty-six), George III (fifty-nine) and Queen Victoria (sixty-three). Although she has faced criticism during her long reign, she has always undertaken her royal duties with great diligence and dignity: 'I cannot lead you into battle. I do not give you laws or administer justice. But I can do something else – I can give my heart and my devotion to these old islands and to all the peoples of our brotherhood of nations.'

Elizabeth was born in 1926 at 17 Bruton Street, London. She was ten years old when her father became king, and she was raised as the heir to the throne from then on. From an early age she had a keen sense of responsibility – she is reported to have once given an officer of the guard permission to march off from her pushchair.

In 1947 she married her third cousin, Prince Philip of Greece and Denmark, who had been living in England since the monarchy had been expelled from Greece. He served in the navy with distinction during the war – he was mentioned in dispatches and rose to become one of the youngest first lieutenants. He and Elizabeth first met in 1939, when he was an eighteen-year-old cadet. They started exchanging letters and gradually fell in love. When they married he renounced his titles, became a British subject and took his mother's name of Mountbatten, converting from Greek Orthodox to Church of England. He is now the longest-serving consort in British history. He is intensely loyal and intelligent, but is prone to hilarious and sometimes offensive gaffes, although this has not harmed his popularity with the British people. Together, Elizabeth and Philip had four children: Charles, Anne, Andrew and Edward.

Elizabeth's coronation in 1953 was the first one to be broadcast to the nation, and many people bought their first television in order to watch it. The royal family found a way of adapting to the new media age that saw the monarchy becoming increasingly popular for a while. The Queen's broadcasts, walkabouts and tireless charitable work, helped by the stately presence of the Queen Mother, helped an outdated institution to survive into the age of the computer.

But as Elizabeth's children grew up, in a less morally restrained age, and hit marital difficulties, the public image of the monarchy began to change. The divorces of three of her four children, and particularly the problems between her eldest son, Charles, and his first wife, Diana, caused the role of the monarchy to be seriously questioned. The almost frenzied media interest in the royals' private troubles threatened to destroy the institution of monarchy altogether. Elizabeth was accused of cold formality in her dealings with her family, particularly with regard to how she dealt with the tragic death of Diana in a car crash in 1997. But the Queen's unswerving devotion to duty seems to have held off the most dangerous of the criticisms.

Some would rather Charles never became king, but a lifetime of public service and a late middle age with his second wife, the dignified Camilla, has restored his reputation and increased his popularity. What does seem clear is that Charles's eldest son, Prince William, has been brought up in the Windsor tradition of quiet, dedicated public service.

The royal family has seen a surge in its popularity in recent years, helped by the public interest in the marriage of Prince William and Catherine Middleton, and support of the Queen's Diamond Jubilee, which was marked by a spectacular tour of the UK and Commonwealth by the Queen and the royal family.

THE MONARCHS OF SCOTLAND

༂

Scotland has a very complicated history of kingship. In the first century Ptolemy described eighteen tribes, each presumably with its own king. Eventually, they converged into the kingdom of Pictland. The Picts (derived from the Roman name for 'painted people') were Britons who spoke the Brythonic dialect of Celtic. There are suggestions that there were seven separate kings in Pictland. Irish Gaels settled in the west and formed the kingdom of Dal Riata (modern-day Argyll, and Bute and Lochaber). North of Hadrian's Wall emerged another kingdom, Alt Clut (later Strathclyde), which was made up mainly of native Britons who had been driven north by the Anglo-Saxon invaders. Scotland emerged when Pictland and Dal Riata came together in the ninth century. Strathclyde was joined to Scotland at around the end of the eleventh century.

A BRIEF HISTORY OF THE ROYAL HOUSES OF SCOTLAND

House of Alpin 843–1034

Founded by Kenneth I MacAlpin, the dynasty saw Scotland go from a collection of warring tribes to a unified kingdom; it ended with Malcolm II.

House of Dunkeld 1034–1286 (or 1290)

Childless, Malcolm II passed the crown to his grandson Duncan I, beginning the House of Dunkeld. Alexander III's death ended it and sparked a succession crisis.

House of Fairhair 1286–90

Disputed because the young Queen Margaret died aged seven, while travelling to Scotland to be crowned.

First interregnum 1290–2

With no obvious ruler, the Guardians of Scotland asked Edward I of England to arbitrate. He agreed, but forced the Scots to swear allegiance to him.

House of Balliol 1292–6

Edward appointed John de Balliol to the throne in 1292, but Edward's attitude to Scotland led John to ally with France.

Second interregnum 1296–1306

Edward invaded, igniting the Scots Wars of Independence. After Wallace's execution, Robert the Bruce claimed power, becoming Robert I in 1306.

House of Bruce 1306–71

In 1307 Edward I died and was succeeded by his weaker son, Edward II. Defeat forced England to accept Scottish independence.

House of Stewart 1371–1567

Robert's son David II succeeded him but died childless. David's nephew Robert Stewart became Robert II, inaugurating Britain's longest-serving royal house, which saw Scotland develop into a modern state.

House of Stuart 1567–1651

When Mary I acceded, she adopted the French form 'Stuart'. From 1603, her son James was also King of England and Ireland (James VI and I). The governments remained separate, but the monarchy was now mainly London-based.

The Commonwealth of England 1652–60

After the English Civil War, Scotland was subsumed into the Commonwealth under Cromwell. The Scots had supported Parliament, but crowned Charles II in 1651, provoking Cromwell's invasion.

House of Stuart restored 1660–1707

After the Restoration, the Kingdom of Scotland was reinstated but its Parliament dissolved. England and Scotland were united by the 1707 Act of Union under Queen Anne, the last monarch of Scotland and of England, and the first of Great Britain.

KENNETH MACALPIN
(CINÁED MAC AILPÍN)
Reigned 843–858/9

By tradition, it is claimed that Kenneth the Conqueror was the first heroic King of Scotland, though he was not called that in his lifetime. His origins are uncertain, but he is said to have become King of Galloway in 834, King of the Gaelic kingdom of Dal Riata in 841 and in 843 he became King of Pictland, thus forming the modern kingdom of Scotland. With claims to both the Pictish and Gaelic thrones, he could unite the two factions into the Kingdom of Alba. His rule of Pictland was contested, but seven years later he arranged a truce at Scone where, according to legend, he murdered his rival, Drest. Kenneth I also supposedly repelled a Viking invasion in 840. He was succeeded by his brother, Donald, and then his son, Constantine I, and his dynasty continued until 1034.

Some modern scholars are unwilling to support the claim that he was the first King of Scotland because there were other kings of Pictland after him and they feel that the two kingdoms of Pictland and Dal Riata gradually merged over the next few generations.

DUNCAN I (DONNCHAD
MAC CRÍNÁIN)
Reigned 1034–1040

Duncan 'the Gracious' came to the throne through his maternal grandfather, Malcolm II. Malcolm had no sons, and seems to have slaughtered the other possible male claimants to the throne. This left the way open to the unopposed accession of his daughter's son, Duncan. Duncan's father was the lay abbot of Dunkeld, and so the new dynasty was called the House of Dunkeld. Duncan's marriage to Suthen, a Northumbrian princess, led people to accuse him of favouring southern ways and his reign is mainly remembered for an infamous rivalry.

A certain Macbeth, Duncan's cousin, was a powerful commander during the reign of Duncan. In 1039 Duncan led a disastrous attack on Durham and in 1040 his army marched into Macbeth's territory in Moray, a region in the north-east, where he was killed by Macbeth, either in battle or murdered at Pitgaveny, near Elgin.

MACBETH (MAC BETHAD MAC FINDLAÍCH)
Reigned 1040–1057

Macbeth was a Gaelic speaker, descended from the kings of Dal Riata. Macbeth's father, Finlay MacRory, was the ruler of Moray until he was murdered by Gillacomgain, who took MacRory's title. Gillacomgain was burnt to death with fifty of his followers, probably by Macbeth, who thus regained Moray. Macbeth married his dead rival's widow, Gruoch, the granddaughter of Kenneth III. Macbeth was also possibly descended from the kings of Scotland, as it is said that his mother might have been the daughter of Malcolm II.

His claim to the throne of Scotland was therefore strong, and following the disasters of King Duncan's reign, Macbeth seized the opportunity to kill the King and take the throne for himself. Contrary to his depiction in Shakespeare's famous play, there is no evidence that Macbeth was particularly evil or weak. Indeed, he ruled well for nearly two decades, imposing a strong sense of law and order, encouraging Christianity and leading successful raids across the border into England. In 1050 he went on a pilgrimage to Rome. At this time, tension was building in England, and exiled Normans, supporters of Edward the Confessor, were settled in Scotland during Macbeth's reign. Macbeth survived an English invasion, but was killed in battle in 1057, by the future Malcolm III, son of Duncan I.

MALCOLM III (MÁEL COLUIM MAC DONNCHADA)
Reigned 1058–1093

Malcolm 'Canmore' (meaning 'great head or chief') was born in 1031, the eldest son of Duncan I. After his father's death at the hands of Macbeth in 1040, Malcolm was sent into exile, probably to England, as there is evidence of a strong Saxon influence in Malcolm's court when he became king. The Saxon language replaced Gaelic as the court language and Malcolm gave some of his children Saxon names.

In 1054 Malcolm defeated Macbeth at Dunsinane, and then again at Lumphanan in 1057, where Macbeth was killed. Macbeth's stepson, Lulach, briefly took the throne until Malcolm murdered him in 1058. He was the second Scottish king known to have been crowned at Scone.

Malcolm married Ingebjorg, the widow of Thorfinn, Earl of

Caithness and the Orkneys, thus securing the north. After the Norman conquest of England, he accepted a lot of exiles, and he took one of them as a second wife – the deeply pious Margaret, granddaughter of Edmund II of England.

Now that he was married into the old Saxon monarchy, Malcolm helped the Saxon cause by attacking Northumbria in support of revolts against William the Conqueror. Eventually he was compelled to swear allegiance to William, but peace with Norman England was short-lived. He also fought against William II and in 1093 he successfully took Alnwick in Northumberland by siege. But while leaning forward to take the keys to the castle from the point of a lance, he was stabbed in the eye and died most painfully. His son Edward was also killed, provoking a conflict over the succession, until Malcolm's brother, Donald III, usurped the throne. Margaret died soon after and was later canonized, becoming Scotland's only royal saint.

ROBERT THE BRUCE (ROBERT I) (ROIBERT A BRIUIS)
Reigned 1306–1329

The royal House of Dunkeld came to an end in 1290, when the brief reign of Margaret (the Maid of Norway, granddaughter of Alexander III) ended with her death by drowning as she crossed to her kingdom. There were thirteen claimants to the throne, including the Bruce family, and Edward I of England was asked to choose between them. Edward chose John Balliol as King of Scotland (1292–1296), but he continued to interfere with Scottish affairs, to the detriment of Balliol's reputation. A council of twelve was forced upon Balliol and they signed a peace treaty with the French, starting the 'Auld Alliance'. Edward invaded, with the support of Robert the Bruce, and defeated the Scots at Dunbar in 1296. Balliol abdicated, and Scotland was left without a king and was ruled by Edward as part of England.

William Wallace led a revolt against the English, and Robert the Bruce switched sides and joined him. Wallace defeated the English at the famous Battle of Stirling Bridge in 1297, but was defeated at Falkirk a year later and Bruce and John Comyn, Balliol's nephew, were appointed 'Guardians of Scotland'. In 1306 Bruce stabbed and killed Comyn during an argument in a church in Dumfries. He was outlawed and excommunicated, but rather than flee, he asserted his right to the throne and was crowned.

But he was soon defeated by Edward I and Comyn's family. Three of his brothers were executed and Bruce fled into exile for a while. In 1307 Edward died and Bruce returned to Scotland and began a highly effective campaign of guerrilla warfare. In 1314 his forces humiliated the English at the Battle of Bannockburn, mainly because of the awful leadership of Edward II. Scotland was declared independent in the Declaration of Arbroath in 1320 and the English signed a peace treaty recognizing Scottish independence in 1328.

Robert the Bruce died a year later, in 1329. His son, David, became king but was overthrown by Edward Balliol, restored again, overthrown again, and finally restored. His grandson, Robert, then became the first Stewart king in 1371, the name coming from his father, Walter Stewart. The dynasty was later renamed Stuart.

JAMES IV
Reigned 1488–1513

James inherited a difficult situation (and much guilt) when his father, the weak and unpopular James III, was killed in a rebellion he himself supported, but he was able to bring Scotland internal peace and the spirit of the Renaissance, and is widely regarded as the most effective of Scotland's Stewart monarchs. An educated polyglot, James was a patron of arts and sciences. Although he improved Scotland's military, his preferred tool was diplomacy, strengthening the Auld Alliance with France. He also sought peace with England (notwithstanding a brief pro-Warbeck invasion in 1496), but when Henry VIII invaded France, James had to take sides. He invaded England in 1513, but was defeated and killed at the Battle of Flodden Field, in which some 10,000 Scots were killed. Scotland subsequently lost the stability James had built.

MARY QUEEN OF SCOTS
Reigned 1542–1567

Mary was vivacious, beautiful and clever, but she also had a lack of judgement that she seems to have passed down to some of her descendants.

She was born in 1542 at Linlithgow Palace, the daughter of Mary of Guise and James V of Scotland. She succeeded her father within seven days of her birth. Her mother was French and Mary was brought up as a Catholic, at a time when most Scots were becoming Protestant. At only six months old, she was betrothed to Henry VIII's son, Edward, but this was repudiated by the Scottish Parliament, so provoking Henry's invasion of Scotland in 1547 (the 'Rough Wooing'). She was then betrothed to the French Dauphin and she was sent to live in France at the age of five. At fifteen she was married to the Dauphin, who became Francis II of France in 1559, but died a year later, aged sixteen. They had no children. She returned to Scotland at the age of eighteen, essentially a French Catholic teenager returning to rule a Protestant country.

For a while, Mary managed to get on with her Protestant lords. But she was ambitious to become Queen of England after Elizabeth I. So, in 1565, she married her first cousin, Henry Stuart, Lord Darnley, which strengthened her position as he had claims to both the Scottish and English thrones. Darnley was handsome but immature, and the marriage was perhaps the mistake that ruined Mary's life. Darnley was manipulated by some of Mary's Protestant lords, who convinced him that Mary was having a relationship with her Italian secretary, David Rizzio, who they said had made her pregnant. Darnley and a party of assassins found Rizzio sheltering behind the Queen. They threatened her with a gun, took Rizzio into a nearby room and stabbed him up to fifty-six times, although some sources say he was killed in front of her. Mary was horrified. At this time, one of her confidants was the rugged Earl of Bothwell, who may also have been her lover. She wrote to him of Darnley: 'Cursed be this poxy fellow that troubleth me this much.' In 1567 the house at Kirk O'Fields where Darnley was staying was blown up and Darnley was found strangled in the garden. Whether or not Mary and Bothwell were involved in the murder is unknown, but they got the blame for it.

It is then claimed that Bothwell kidnapped and raped Mary

and forced her to marry him, though some say that she was a willing participant. The horrified Protestant lords had had enough. They imprisoned Mary and exiled Bothwell, and she was forced to abdicate in favour of her son with Darnley (James VI of Scotland and later James I of England), who was taken away from her and brought up as a Protestant. She was still only twenty-four, and she spent the rest of her life imprisoned, first by the Scots and then, after leading a failed rebellion and fleeing to to England, by the English. She was executed in 1587, on Elizabeth I's orders, for her alleged involvement in a Catholic plot to usurp the throne of England. In 1603, Elizabeth's death led to the Union of the Crowns – James succeeded his mother to rule both Scotland and England.

KINGS OF WALES

❧

Wales has not been an independent entity for much of its history. Until the coming of the Saxons, it was in no sense distinct from 'England', as it would become, and indeed was under military rule along with much of the rest of Britain during the Roman period. After the Romans left, native groupings slowly re-emerged in the face of threats from the Saxons and then the Normans. There were local kings, but as far as can be discovered there were no kings of Wales until Wales was cut off from the rest of Britain by the Saxons, when King Offa built his great dyke in the eighth century. The name 'Wales' in fact derives from the Saxons, who called the natives 'the Welsh', meaning strangers. Eventually, as pressure from the English increased, the Welsh kingdoms were united briefly, before Welsh independence was extinguished by King Edward I in the thirteenth century.

CUNEDDA WLEDIG AP EDERN
Reigned *c.* 450–460

Cunedda (or Kenneth) means 'good lord'. Cunedda seems to have been descended from a Roman land-owning official. He was given the title of Wledig (meaning 'holder of lands'), which is shared with only a few other early Welsh kings and Magnus Maximus, who was declared Roman Emperor in Britain. Possibly under orders from Maximus Vortigern in the fifth century, Cunedda and his people were moved from their ancestral home north of Hadrian's Wall to northern Wales (founding the Kingdom of Gwnedd), apparently to defend Britain from the marauding Irish. The powerful Gwynedd dynasty was thus founded and would last until Welsh independence was lost in the thirteenth century.

CADWALADR FENDIGAID
AP CADWALLON
Reigned *c.* 655–682

Cadwallader the Blessed was born in around 632. He was King of Gwynedd, but supposedly also claimed the role of High King of Britain. He is said to have been the last king to make a serious attempt to stem the inexorable advance of the Saxons. He attacked the Saxons in Somerset without lasting effect and spent the rest of his reign in Wales establishing monasteries. The Welsh treated him as a saint, although he was never officially canonized.

His standard depicted a red dragon, which became the symbol of Henry Tudor and is on the national flag of Wales; Henry himself was keen to be seen as the embodiment of the spirit of Cadwallader.

RHODRI MAWR AP MERFYN
Reigned 844–878

Rhodri the Great was the first king to rule the majority of Wales. He achieved this through dynastic marriage and military power. His father was King of Gwynedd and when his mother's uncle died he also inherited Powys in the east. In 872 his wife Angharad's brother drowned and Rhodri added Seisyllwg in southern Wales to his kingdom. Rhodri is remembered for a famous victory against the Vikings in 856, when he killed the Danish leader, Gorm. In 878 he clashed with Alfred the Great of England and was killed.

HYWEL DDA AP CADELL
Reigned 942–950

Hywel the Good was the grandson of Rhodri the Great and son of Cadell of Deheubarth. Hywel was born around 880 and became King of Dyfed in the south-west, which was conquered by Cadell and granted by marriage, in 905. After his cousin, Idwal Foel, died in 942, he seized power in Gwynedd. He adopted a policy of peace with the Saxons, forming an alliance with Athelstan of England. The Welsh did not therefore join the alliance of anti-English kings that was defeated by Athelstan at the Battle of Brunanburh in 937.

Hywel was very well educated and went on a pilgrimage to

Rome. Although his kingdom split again after his death, his codification of Welsh laws was a unifying factor in the foundation of the Welsh legal system until it was abolished by the English in the sixteenth century.

GRUFFYDD AP LLYWELYN
Reigned 1039–1063 (Ruled over all Wales 1051–1063)

Gruffydd is the only king to have controlled the whole of Wales. He was already King of Powys when he usurped the throne of Gwynedd in 1039 after the incumbent was killed, possibly on Gruffydd's orders. He defeated an English army near Welshpool on the River Severn, killing the brother of the Earl of Mercia and then defeated Hywel ab Edwin, the great-grandson of Hywel Dda, and married his wife. After several setbacks, he defeated Hywel's successor and gained Deheubarth (Seisyllwg and Dyfed). In 1055 he allied himself with Ælfgār, ex-Earl of Mercia and enemy of Harold Godwinson (Harold II), burnt down Hereford and incorporated Gwent in the south-east into his kingdom, thus becoming king of all of Wales from 1057 to 1063. He was described as 'prodigal, watchful, active, bold, quick-witted, affable, lecherous, wicked, treacherous, and pitiless'.

Finally, after Ælfgār's death Harold Godwinson, helped by his brother Tostig, took Gruffydd on and forced him to retreat to Snowdonia, where he was murdered by one of his own men.

OWAIN GWYNEDD AP GRUFFYDD
Reigned 1137–1170

Owain was born in around 1100. From 1120 he fought with his brothers against the Normans, who were looking to expand their territories into Wales. In 1137 he inherited Gwynedd from his father. Initially he shared the kingdom with his brother Cadwalladr, but in 1143 Cadwalladr was implicated in a murder and Owain ruled alone from then on. He expanded the borders of Gwynedd to the east while England was powerless during the anarchy brought by the civil war of King Stephen's reign. In 1157, Henry II invaded, aided by Cadwalladr, and although Owain defeated Henry on Anglesey, a truce was agreed in which Owain had to cede his newly conquered lands, although he later retook them.

In 1163 Owain made a truce with the ruler of Deheubarth, Rhys ap Gruffudd, uniting the Welsh in an alliance. In 1165 Henry II invaded again, but the terrible Welsh weather enabled the united Welsh to avoid a pitched battle and send a frustrated Henry back home.

Owain made an alliance with the King of France and was able to retain Welsh independence during his lifetime. Castles and monasteries were built and the Welsh state developed in the relatively peaceful years of Owain's reign.

LLYWELYN FAWR AP IORWERTH
Reigned 1195–1240

Llywelyn the Great was the grandson of Owain Gwynedd and, like him, was a great leader who dominated Wales and kept the English at bay.

He was born in 1173 and at the age of fifteen may have already have been at war with his uncles Daffyd and Rhodri ab Owain, who had divided Gwynedd between them. When he became ruler in 1200, he made a treaty of loyalty to King John and then sealed the relationship by marrying John's illegitimate daughter, Joan. In 1209 he fought for John against the Scots, and in Wales annexed lands in south Powys.

He soon fell out with John, however, and an English invasion aided by other Welsh princes in 1211 forced him to retreat to Snowdonia. He sent his wife to make peace with John, which ended the war but cost him land on his eastern border. But by clever alliances with Welsh princes, the King of France and the barons who had forced John to sign the Magna Carta, he consolidated his position as the unopposed leader of Wales, driving the English from North Wales and taking Shrewsbury in 1215.

Following the death of King John in 1216, Llywelyn signed a peace treaty with Henry III, but for the next few years he fought a series of campaigns against the Norman lords in the borders of Wales. In 1230 William de Braose, of Abergavenny, visiting to arrange a marriage between his daughter and Llywelyn's son Dafydd, was found alone in a room with Llywelyn's wife. William was hanged and Joan placed under house arrest. She was forgiven after a year of disgrace.

In 1234 a further peace treaty was made with England, which was sustained until the end of Llywelyn's life. In 1237 he suffered a stroke and his son Daffydd took over the reins. He died peacefully in 1240.

DAFYDD AP LLYWELYN
Reigned 1240–1246

Dafydd was the legitimate son of Llywelyn the Great, but Llywelyn had an older illegitimate son, Gruffydd, who enjoyed wide support. In Welsh law, illegitimate children had rights of inheritance if acknowledged by their father. Llywelyn, however, went out of his way to ensure that Dafydd became king, although he began to use the style 'Prince of Wales'.

In 1241, when Dafydd showed signs of planning an alliance with Louis IX of France (Saint Louis), Henry III invaded Gwynedd, and to secure peace Dafydd had to surrender all his territories outside of Gwynedd and hand over his elder half-brother, Gruffydd, to Henry. Gruffydd was kept in the Tower of London but attempted to escape by knotting sheets together to make a rope. Unfortunately it broke and he fell to his death. With the hostage dead, Dafydd could ally himself to other Welsh princes to attack English possessions. In 1245 Henry invaded again and met stiff resistance from Dafydd. A truce was agreed, but Dafydd died suddenly in 1246. With no heir, Gruffydd's sons took power.

LLYWELYN AP GRUFFYDD (LLYWELYN EIN LLYW OLAF – LLYWELN, OUR LAST LEADER)
Reigned 1246–1282

Llywelyn the Last was the last native Prince of Wales before Wales was conquered and subjugated to England by Edward I. When Dafydd ap Llywelyn died without an heir in 1246, Henry

III allowed Dafydd's nephews, Llywelyn and Owain, to rule western Gwynedd jointly, although he took their eastern lands. When their younger brother Dafydd came of age, Henry announced that he too was to have a share of the kingdom. Llywelyn refused to give up more land and his brothers allied themselves against him, but he defeated them in 1255 at the Battle of Bryn Derwin.

Llywelyn soon managed to reclaim eastern Gwynedd (whose people resented occupation) and began expanding south. He allied himself with Simon de Montfort against Henry III, and after the defeat of de Montfort, he agreed a treaty with Henry in 1267 that saw him acknowledged as Prince of Wales.

But this was the high point of his reign. He stopped paying the tribute demanded by the treaty and arranged a marriage with de Montfort's daughter, Eleanor. This provoked the new King, Edward I, into an overwhelming English invasion in 1277 and the enforcement of a peace treaty that saw Llywelyn pushed back to north-west Gwynedd.

In 1282 Llywelyn's brother Dafydd provoked a Welsh revolt, which Llywelyn felt obliged to support. Llywelyn was killed in an attack at Orewin Bridge. His head was taken to London and stuck on a gate at the Tower of London, where it remained for fifteen years. Dafydd attempted to continue the war, but Edward's forces constructed a ring of massive fortresses, dismantled the Welsh principalities and brought Wales under English rule.

FURTHER READING

1066: The Year of the Three Battles, F.J. McLynn, Jonathan Cape Ltd, 1998

A Brief History of the Anglo-Saxons, Geoffrey Hindley, Robinson Publishing, 2006

A History of the English Church and People, Bede Venerabilis, Penguin Classics, 1955

A History of Britain, Simon Schama, BBC Books, 2000

An Utterly Impartial History of Britain, John O'Farrell, Black Swan, 2008

Britain AD, Francis Pryor, HarperCollins, 2004

Britain and the End of the Roman Empire, Ken Dark, Tempus, 2000

Elizabeth, David Starkey, Vintage, 2001

Empire: How Britain Made the Modern World, Niall Ferguson, Penguin, 2004

Faith and Treason: The Story of the Gunpowder Plot, Antonia Fraser, Anchor Books, 1997

Kings and Queens of Early Britain, Geoffrey Ashe, Methuen, 2000

Queen Victoria: A Personal History, Christopher Hibbert, HarperCollins, 2001

The History of the Kings of Britain, Geoffrey of Monmouth, translated by Lewis Thorpe, Penguin Classics, 2004

The Isles, Norman Davies, Macmillan, 1999

The Myth of the Blitz, Angus Calder, Jonathan Cape Ltd, 1991

The Origins of the British: A Genetic Detective Story, Stephen Oppenheimer, Carroll & Graf Publishing, 2006

The Princes in the Tower, Alison Weir, The Bodley Head Ltd, 1992

The Six Wives of Henry VIII, Alison Weir, Vintage, 2007

Who's Who in British History, Juliet Gardiner, Collins & Brown, 2002

INDEX